PATHWAYS
TO A
DECISION
WITH IGNATIUS OF LOYOLA

JIM MAHER SJ

ISBN 978 1 78812 270 2

Designed by Messenger Publications Design Department
Typeset in Adobe Caslon Pro & Academy Engraved
Cover image: Teo Tarras / Shutterstock
Printed by Johnswood Press Limited

Messenger Publications,
37 Leeson Place, Dublin D02 E5V0
www.messenger.ie

CONTENTS

INTRODUCTION

'What's the difference between the Jesuits and other religious orders? What does AMDG mean?' Such questions were not unusual during more than thirty years' teaching in a Jesuit comprehensive school in Limerick. They showed that the students were noticing and thinking. Thousands of people in Ireland, and countless numbers in other countries, were educated by the Jesuits. Jesuit schools welcome not just the students into the fold, but also staff, parents, alumni, boards of management personnel and many others. However, Jesuit outreach also includes many other types of activity apart from education. All over the globe Jesuit communities can be found running parishes, refugee and social service centres and communication networks. They lead retreats and pilgrimages. They support indigenous peoples and advocate for climate justice. They reach out to prisoners, the homeless and others on the margins, and provide a variety of other services that promote a faith that does justice. Jesuits do this as an expression of gratitude for what they have received and – influenced by the spirituality of St Ignatius – in response to the invitation of Jesus to us to wash one another's feet.

Of course the Jesuits never would have existed except for an unexpected collision. A French cannon ball ripped through the air in the Spanish town of Pamplona on 20 May 1521. A thirty-year-old Basque nobleman, Ignatius from Loyola, was standing in its trajectory, defending the Spanish garrison from the ramparts. The cannon ball shattered not only Ignatius's legs but also his dream of being a great soldier. His career path was in ruins. Paradoxically, the 'gift!' of an unwanted cannon ball was the catalyst that would eventually change his life for the better. This concurrence – Ignatius in the way and the cannon ball ripping through the air – was God's way of battering Ignatius's heart, as in John Donne's poem 'Batter my heart', when he says: 'Batter my heart, three person'd God, for you / As yet but knock, breathe, shine, and seek to mend; / … and bend / Your force to break, blow, burn and make me new.' Coincidentally, this was also the realisation of a premonition of Ignatius's aunt Marina, a nun, who on one occasion said to him, 'Inigo, you will not learn nor become wise until someone breaks your leg.'[1] This Pamplona moment has the hallmarks of God's presence working in mysterious and, from Ignatius's viewpoint, unwanted ways! Apparent coincidence can be God's way of breaking into our lives for good.

Over thirty years of working with young people has confirmed for this author that there is an enormous welcome for the wisdom of Ignatius of Loyola whose spirituality inspires the Jesuits. Students are eager to embrace Ignatian wisdom as expressed in *The Characteristics of Jesuit Education*[2] and *Jesuit Schools: A Living Tradition in the 21st Century*.[3] They welcome retreats, school masses, student and/or teacher-led morning prayer, social outreach experiences, peer-led retreats and even challenging pilgrimages such as the Quo Vadis, Lourdes or Santiago de Compostela experience. It is encouraging to have so many students who are willing to step up to the plate in order to become ministers of the Eucharist, readers at school liturgies and to lead the prayers at the beginning of the regular assemblies of close to a thousand students and staff. In more recent times the Ignatian Examen of Consciousness prayer has begun to take root among students in many parts of the world as a concrete response to a conference of Jesuit education delegates in 2017.

1   José Ignacio Tellechea Idigoras, Trans. Cornelius Michael Buckley SJ, *Ignatius of Loyola – The Pilgrim Saint,* Chicago, IL: Loyola Press, 1994, 72.
2   ICAJE, 1986.
3   The International Commission on the Apostolate on Jesuit Education, Rome: Society of Jesus, 2019.

This prayer form is dealt with in Chapter 6. Students are encouraged to reflect on the meaning of their life experiences through the lens of Ignatian wisdom.

Of course, much of this would not be possible without the support of parents, staff and others. Ignatian wisdom has the knack of touching the heart of any age group because it starts with where people are at and acknowledges that no two people travel on the same path to God. Ignatian wisdom rejects the straightjacket approach to spirituality. It affirms the individual's unique worth as God's particular work of art, while at the same time challenging the person to own who they are and to contribute to the beauty and the joy of the world by being the 'self' that God intended them to be. Summing up a central idea of the Jesuit poet, Gerard Manley Hopkins, this can be expressed as: 'I am I because God wants me to be me.'[4] This way of reverencing the individual is expressed in Jesuit circles through what's called '*cura personalis*', care of the individual.

However, while many people admire the Jesuits and have some familiarity with Ignatian wisdom, experience tells me there are many associated with Jesuit works who don't know much about Ignatian wisdom and would like to know more about the basics. The purpose of this book is to present some of the key ideas of Ignatius's spirituality in an accessible way. This is not an academic tome. The book is laced with poetic references because poetry has the knack of invading the spirit by getting under the intellectual radar and nourishing the heart. For those who already know a lot, this book will serve as a revision course! And as many already know, Ignatian repetition – going back to where our hearts were stirred – is an important strategy to deepen our perceptions.

For those who want to learn more, this book will provide the basics and enough to be getting on with in the pursuit of a spiritual life inspired by Ignatius. It will be helpful for parents of students in Jesuit schools and colleges, older students, staff, alumni and others to read this

4 Margaret R. Ellsberg (ed.), *The Gospel in Gerard Manley Hopkins*, New York, NY: Plough Publishing House, 2017, 90.

book to learn more about what influences the Jesuit ethos and for the development of their own spiritual practices. This book is also intended for a much wider readership. Anyone at all interested in the Jesuits will find it a helpful introduction to understanding a little more about how Jesuits tick.

This book highlights Ignatius's understanding of where we have come from and where we are going to. It is one individual's faith narrative, which may inspire our own quest for faith or reignite the smouldering ashes of a faith we grew out of. He shares his rich understanding of what life is about in his most famous written text, *The Spiritual Exercises* (SE), and his other writings, such as his *Autobiography* and his many letters. He experienced how we can get trapped in thoughts and feelings that prevent us realising our full potential, which is sometimes only unleashed through a metaphorical or real cannon ball, or when God invades the heart with a battering ram, as in the case of the poet John Donne.

Ignatius gives us helpful practical guidelines on how to interpret our moods so that we can live life to the full, making the most of the many gifts we have been given. He encourages us to discover who we really are and what we really want from life. He wants us, in the words of the poet Walt Whitman, to 'weave the song of myself'. Ignatius, also conscious of how much we receive from the hands of a loving God through the circumstances of life, gets us to consider the most appropriate ways to give back some of what we have been given by supporting our fellow travellers on life's path, especially those weakened by the challenges of the journey.

To help us do this he has given sound advice on how to make good decisions, unimpaired by blind spots, in so far as that is possible in this life. Robert Frost's much-loved poem 'The Road Not Taken' resonates with people because it highlights the complexity of making life-decisions. One major choice precludes other choices. All of us at some stage, especially young people leaving school or college, or older people having to reconstruct their lives, have to make serious decisions about their future. Many of us would like to keep as many options open as possible. But Frost points out that that's not possible, employing the imagery of a person having to make a choice at a fork on an autumn woodland path. 'Two roads diverged in a yellow wood, / And sorry I could not travel both / And be one traveler.' We can't have it both ways. We need to make up our minds about one or the other.

Chapters 8 and 9 are given over to Ignatius's guidelines on decision-making in the hope that we make the right decisions, like Robert Frost, for whom the road 'was not only the "different" road, the right road for him, but the only road he could have taken'.[5] The challenge for us all is to make decisions which help us to express who we really are. This is where Ignatius comes into his own, sharing wisdom which facilitates the channelling of all that's best in us, so that our lives, echoing Gerard Manley Hopkins, cry out: '*What I do is me: for that I came*' ('As Kingfishers Catch Fire').

Life is never straightforward! This is well illustrated in the Robert Burns poem 'To A Mouse', written in his Scottish highland dialect on the occasion of a plough destroying a mouse's nest, which in turn inspired the immortal lines: 'The best-laid schemes o' mice an' men / Gang aft agley, / An' lea'e us nought but grief an' pain, / For promis'd joy!' The resonant phrase 'gang aft agley' refers to something going awry or going wrong, an experience with which we can easily identify. Sometimes, for every step forward, there are two steps backwards. There will be times of bewilderment and disappointment when we find ourselves in the middle of storms that will distort our vision and lead us down the wrong path. The final chapter is an encouragement to stay the course by sticking to the right path, following the Ignatian advice highlighted in this book. It suggests discovering regular oasis moments suited to where we find ourselves in order to water the seeds of the Ignatian principles that I hope this book will have sown.

5   *New Enlarged Anthology of Robert Frost's Poems*, with introduction and commentary by Louis Untermeyer, New York, NY: Washington Square Press, 1971, 22.

As we pursue our own unique path, making our own distinctive contribution as God intended, we do so drawing confidence from the eighth-century Celtic prayer, 'The Deer's Cry'. 'I arise today / Through God's strength to pilot me: / God's might to uphold me, / God's wisdom to guide me.' In the town of Triacastela, located on the pilgrim trail to Santiago de Compostela, the local parish priest gives good advice to pilgrims: 'Remember God doesn't count your steps or Santiago weigh your pack – what they measure is your heart, pilgrim, so look to your heart … and take care of your feet!'[6] As you read this book, it's hard to come up with a better suggestion. 'Look to your heart … and take care of your feet!' as you come to grips with what makes Jesuits different from others and as you mull over how AMDG (*Ad Majorem Dei Gloriam*, 'for the greater glory of God') might impact your life. *Go gcuire Dia ar ár leas sinn agus go stiúra Dia sinn*! (May God put us on the right road and guide us!)

6   *Camino to Santiago: A Spiritual Companion*, Chawton: Redemptorist Publications, 2016, 33.

WHAT'S IT ALL ABOUT?

Imagine the first human beings. Over thousands of years they have emerged from the slime of the earth and learned to stand upright on their own two feet. At first, their days were spent hunting, eating, sleeping, and procreating. Their preoccupation was survival. Over time, having taken in every detail of their environment, they began to ask questions. Something had clicked in their brains, generating a new kind of curiosity. Abstract questions were beginning to surface as they gathered together in the evening time reminiscing about the day's activities. A central question was increasingly coming to the fore – 'What's it all about?' They had other equally probing questions, such as 'Why is there something rather than nothing?' 'Where are we going to?' Those questions are still asked by each generation as it struggles with the meaning of life.

These developing humans would also have spotted something within themselves that they couldn't quite grasp. A battle in their hearts was drawing them this way and that in opposite directions. This, too, is an experience with which every generation can identify. A popular and helpful image that highlights this internal conflict is found in the Cherokee story of the two wolves.

An elderly grandfather tells his grandson that within the heart of every person there are two wolves fighting for our spirit. One is good and one is evil. The good wolf has all the positive attributes of peace, joy, gentleness, compassion and all the other good qualities we can think of. On the other hand, the bad wolf is arrogant, deceptive, proud and narcissistic. He has all the bad features we can think of.

The grandson shivers a little as he thinks about these two wolves trying to spirit him away. He asks his grandfather the important question: 'Granddad, which wolf wins?' The grandfather replies by telling his grandson that it's the wolf you feed! What we feed the wolves is important because they become what they eat. If we don't reflect about things, we can unconsciously feed the bad wolf, the bad spirit, who will sneak up to bite us.

St Ignatius Loyola is the fearless wolf whisperer par excellence! Since the day he could see for the first time, he would have noticed two upright wolves on the family crest around a cooking pot. The family name Loyola is derived from this image of a wolf (*lobo*), Y (and), a cooking pot (*olla*). Therefore, we get LO (as in *lobo*), Y (and), and OLA (as in *olla*). LO+Y+OLA = LOYOLA

In hindsight the two wolves are somewhat ironic. Their inclusion on the Loyola family crest was inspired by a popular story recounting how Ignatius's ancestors would generously feed all and sundry, including wolves, after their sumptuous banquets. The wolf motif is included to highlight the Loyola generosity.

Ignatius's paternal grandfather, Juan Pérez de Oñaz, in pursuit of prestige and status, would metaphorically feed the bad wolf, stirring up local feuds to remind everyone who was the local regional boss. His was a life driven by a lust for power. His grandson, Ignatius, would spend half his life supporting others in the process of deciding if the idolisation of power, prestige, status and the acquisition of material possessions really expressed their core values. Perhaps there was more to life than what was dictated by the unexamined conventional wisdom. Maybe there was a gentler and more satisfying diet for the wolves.

Juan Pérez could never have imagined that his grandson would be a famous wolf whisperer, sharing his gift with countless people, taming what Ignatius would call their 'disordered affections', represented by the bad wolf, otherwise known as the bad spirit, 'the enemy of our human nature'. These 'disordered affections' are all those energies that deflect us from our true selves, all those tendencies that distract us from the richness of experiencing what it is to be human at its most authentic. The wolf whisperer urges us to embrace what helps us attain our goal of growing into our own unique personhood and to surrender what impedes it. Be wary of what you feed the wolves, because the best-fed wolf wins the battle and grows so big that the other wolf is squeezed out. When we give in to discouragement, self-preoccupation, cut ourselves off from others, welcome resentment and nurture other life-denying behaviours, it's like feeding the bad wolf its favourite food. Ignatius cautions us, like the Cherokee chief, to pay attention to what's going on in the cauldron of our hearts, because, as on the Loyola family crest, the two wolves, on their hind legs, are waiting to be fed.

Ignatius Loyola was born in 1491. In 1492 Christopher Columbus reached the shores of the New World. Ignatius's parents had been married for twenty-four years when Ignatius was born. He was the youngest of thirteen siblings – six boys, four girls, and two step-sisters, born of his father's extra-marital affairs. His mother died when he was a child, and his father died when Ignatius was sixteen, shortly after he had left home to take up a position at the royal treasury.

Like the rest of us Ignatius struggled with the 'What's it all about?' question and the conflict between the good wolf and the bad wolf that is played out every day in our hearts. His answers shaped his life and the lives of countless others. He went on to become the founder, with others, of the Society of Jesus, commonly referred to as the Jesuits. He was an unconventional saint and in his early life was certainly not saint material – far from it! Perhaps we can take hope from his tale of conversion. We don't need to be imprisoned or defined by our past.

Like many of his generation Ignatius was a cradle Catholic whose religion was driven more by convention than conviction. One of the early Jesuits remarked: 'Though he was attached to the faith, he lived no wise in conformity with it and did not avoid sin'.[7] He was vain and he was ambitious like his granddad, Juan Pérez. He was 'addicted to gambling and dissolute in his dealings with women, contentious and keen about using his sword'.[8] He was in every way his father's son and the Loyola machismo was ingrained in his DNA. He enjoyed wild parties. In his own words, he also 'delighted especially in the exercise of arms' at the duels and tournaments that were customary at the time.

He wasn't exactly the model of a good Catholic boy – quite the opposite, and at its very worst extreme! He was driven by ego and the intense desire to make a name for himself at the highest rung of the social ladder. He was not a politically correct twenty-first-century male. Ignatius is best understood against his social and cultural background, many aspects of which would not be tolerated today. His was a life charged with intensely ambiguous and powerful energies inherited from his culture, which providentially would come under the microscope to be rechannelled in a totally different direction.

There is some compelling evidence he fathered a child during a romantic interlude. As reputable a source as Cardinal Carlo Martini SJ remarks that 'This detail was brought to light after the discovery of certain documents which probably had been deliberately side-tracked by the early Jesuits'.[9] This is a credible assessment of the Jesuit mentality of the time. Ignatius already had enough scandalous skeletons in his closet without the need for another one! There is also a suggestion in Ignatius's autobiography that this story is true, when he says that once when he had received money that was owed to him from his employer 'he sent it to some persons toward whom he had certain obligations'. There is a suggestion here that he made financial arrangements for

7   W. W. Meissner, *Ignatius of Loyola: The Psychology of a Saint*, Newhaven, CT, and London: Yale University Press, 1992, 25.
8   Ibid.
9   Cardinal Carlo Martini SJ, *Letting God Free Us*, Slough and New York, NY: St Pauls and New City Press, 1993, 44.

the support of his daughter equivalent to having her adopted. At least he took responsibility for his actions on this occasion, unlike when he got himself into trouble with the law in connection with a brawl on Shrove Tuesday 1515. Evidence of this incident is still in the public domain. How many other saints have left behind such a legacy? After the event Ignatius hotfooted it from Loyola to Pamplona to evade the legal consequences. As luck would have it, arguments about legal technicalities seem to have undermined the prosecution's case.

As a teenager Ignatius was apprenticed to the Spanish treasury department. He moved in the most influential social circles, living in an opulent and luxurious household while networking with the movers and shakers, the great and the good. He would have met the king on a number of occasions. He wore the most elegant, fashionable and expensive clothes. He had a fine head of hair which he groomed meticulously. By all accounts he was a handsome young man, and many women worshipped the ground he walked on. He loved music. He had a bright future ahead of him. His was a 'charmed life'. His career trajectory was marked out for him.

Ignatius had some military experience, having fought twice on the front line. But his stubbornness and impetuosity dramatically changed the course of his life. His biggest moment on the battlefield came when the French and Spanish were at war in Pamplona, Spain, in May 1521. It was clear that victory was beyond the grasp of the Spanish. However, Ignatius, stubborn, passionate, loyal and immensely courageous, insisted that the battle be fought to the death. He was struck in both legs by a French cannonball. His right leg was badly broken and he had to return home to Loyola, where he spent the best part of a year recuperating from his double surgery. He wasn't pleased with the first procedure the doctors performed on his leg. It left him with a limp and a piece of bone jutting out. Not only would this not go down well with the ladies, it would prevent him from wearing the most fashionable attire from the waist down. His vanity dictated that the doctors saw off the protruding bone, which they did. With no recourse to anaesthesia it's no wonder he nearly lost his life, traumatised by such 'butchery', the apt term he uses in his autobiography. This fierce and lopsided tenacity tells us so much about Ignatius. These events provide a window on his vanity, determination, heroism and loyalty to king and country.

The turning point of his life came during his long recuperation while sifting through the differences in his feelings in response to daydreaming and reading books. After his long daydreams of his imaginary future exploits and the reputation he would make for himself as a man of the world, he noticed he felt empty and listless. Such daydreams just didn't hit the spot. The only books in his family's castle were a *Life of Christ* and the biographies of saints, which were not exactly his cup of tea. Tales of knights in shining armour and amorous and beautiful young women were more to his liking than St Francis, St Dominic or any other saint. How dull they were! He needed any distraction to while away the daily tedium of being bedridden. Surprisingly, his affective response to his reading of the lives of the saints, on the other hand, inspired him to follow another direction. His pride and vanity were reasserting themselves. 'I can do better than those saints I've read about!'

Over time he concluded that God communicates his hopes for us through our desires, feelings and thoughts. This is Ignatius's fundamental legacy to all those searching for meaning and direction in their lives. He stressed the importance of listening to what's going on in our hearts and he gave us directions to help interpret the ebb and flow of our feelings, desires and thoughts. His long convalescence was a blessing in disguise. It gave him the opportunity to uncover the many different layers of his personality and get to the core of who he was. Through this long, arduous and physically painful process he began to discover there was more to life than met the eye. He began to get in touch with who he really was and what he genuinely wanted out of life. He was able to unearth the real man at the core of his personality; the one beyond the gambling, the promiscuity, the pride, the ambition and the arrogance. Up to this time, and unknown to himself, the bad wolf had been gradually squeezing out the good wolf, but this would soon stop. The long period of reflection translated itself into a practical decision.

At the end of the nine-month recuperation process during which he was reborn, Ignatius left home for good in February 1522 to serve God as a layperson, in Jerusalem or elsewhere. The next stage of his spiritual journey was not what he expected. First, he went to his former employer to collect money owed to him. He then made his way to the famous monastery of Montserrat, where the icon of the Black Madonna still has pride of place. It took him three days to confess his sins as he wanted to write down everything. He hung up his weapons near the statue of the Madonna as a symbol of the rejection of his former ambitions and a sign of his desire to live simply as a pilgrim for the rest of his life. The complex energies that drove him in the past would now be rechannelled in the opposite direction of what he had originally planned for his life. All that bubbling energy would be harnessed in the service of God.

He then moved down the mountain to the nearby town of Manresa, east of Barcelona, where he spent the most part of a year, making regular use of a cave, which has been preserved, while accepting the hospitality of the Dominican friars, a local hospice and others who provided food and lodging. At one point he contemplated ending his own life, such was the intensity of his shame and self-loathing about his former life. He experienced disturbing suicidal depression arising from fears that his sins had not been forgiven because he hadn't confessed them properly. He recognised how seriously disordered and egotistical his past life had been. He was in a dark place inspired by the bad spirit who works to intensify our most disturbing fears and anxieties. His physical appearance matched his inner turmoil. The once immaculately groomed hair was now unwashed and unkempt. His nails were uncut. He no longer wore the fashionable and expensive clothes that were de rigueur for the young men of his social class. He was a sorry sight as he begged in the streets of Manresa.

He sought peace by doing what is unhelpful. He kept repeating his confessions, an unhealthy habit that merely served to reinforce his anxieties. At this stage he had not yet come to experience the tender mercy of God and the realisation that sacramental confession is not intended to be, as Pope Francis says, a 'torture chamber'. It took him some time to realise that his negative thoughts were coming from the bad spirit who had distorted his perceptions and loosened his grasp on reality to a point where he had lost the capacity to make good decisions. He would learn in time that in such situations the good spirit leads us gently and firmly to fuller self-integration. He would come to distinguish between neurotic and creative guilt.

At this time Ignatius kept a notebook in which he recorded his inner life. For such an energetic, gregarious and complex character he was an astute observer and interpreter of the inner dynamics of the spirit, his desires, his feelings and moods. He didn't have the lingo of contemporary psychology even though he was practising cognitive behavioural therapy before it was invented! While at Manresa he had one of the most significant religious experiences of his life on the banks of the River Cardoner, which enabled him to see everything in a new light – 'the eyes of his understanding began to be opened'.[10] This experience restored his confidence and was a driving force for the rest of his life.

This period of his life came to an end in February 1523 when he began his long and arduous journey to Jerusalem, where he eventually arrived on 4 September. Owing to the political tensions of the time he was sent packing by the Franciscan in charge of the holy places under threat of excommunication. The stubborn Ignatius reluctantly complied, but before he left he had the opportunity to visit the places that meant so much to him.

In the course of time his Spiritual Exercises saw the light of day and the booklet was circulated among a small group. It was to become a

10   Referenced in *The Autobiography of St Ignatius Loyola*, Joseph F. O'Callaghan (trans.), John C. Olin (ed.), New York, NY: Harper torch Books, 1974, 39.

classic of spirituality, a manual for accompanying others in their spiritual quest inspired by his own experience. It is the reference manual for retreats based on the wisdom of Ignatius. It is not a book for bedtime reading. Like instruction manuals in other disciplines, the 'exercises' are meant to be done, but in this case preferably with the support of an experienced person who is familiar with the dynamics and movements of Ignatius's method.

Even if the idea of Ignatian retreats does not appeal to us, or are not possible for us, it's helpful to remember that many of Ignatius's insights are enormously helpful when adapted to ordinary life, especially in decision making and interpreting our feelings, which are at the root of good and bad moods. Even though Ignatius's insights owe their origin to a specifically spiritual context, the inherent principles can be applied more universally, as the experience of countless numbers of people confirms.

FIRST THINGS FIRST

In his 'Principle and Foundation', a reflection at the beginning of his Spiritual Exercises, Ignatius sums up his worldview by answering the 'What's it all about?' question. He found his own answer to the universal existential homesickness. Of course, Ignatius wasn't the first to articulate an answer to the question. Philosophers and others had done so long before he arrived on the scene. Biblical authors had eloquently expressed what we're really looking for, as, for example, in Psalm 26: 'There is one thing I ask of the Lord, / For this I long, / To live in the house of the Lord, / All the days of my life, / To savour the sweetness of the Lord, / To behold his holy temple.' This deep longing for God and all that God stands for, such as beauty, truth, justice, mercy and love, has already been sown in our hearts by God. Our internal GPS is fixed on God. It's our fundamental orientation in life. It's simply a fact of our existence. Some of us are more conscious of this reality than others, for a variety of complex cultural, spiritual and personal factors that influence our outlook. We need a sense of wonder to discover the fundamental reality of who we are.

This basic longing of the heart is also echoed in the famous prayer of St Augustine, who, like Ignatius, was no model of virtue in his early life and came late to religion. 'You have made us for yourself, O Lord, and our hearts are restless until they repose in you.' These two ideas are blended together in Ignatius's map for life, which he called the 'Principle and Foundation'.

> God wants to share life and love with us for ever. Our loving response to God's friendship is expressed when we embrace life in all its fullness and goodness. We express our gratitude to God by serving others and using the gifts God has given us. We embrace the gifts that help us in our friendship with God and surrender those that don't. All created reality is a gift of God to help us encounter God in this life and the life to come. We respect God's gifts by using them to the best of our abilities and in that way advance God's plan and intention for our world.' (Adapted from SE, 23)

For Ignatius the primary reason for the existence of human beings is to embrace life in all its fullness and goodness. This is how we welcome God into our lives and respond to his generosity. It's in our genes to be in a relationship with God; we share the spiritual genetic make-up of Jesus, our own flesh and blood, by virtue of his sharing in our human experience. The metaphor of longing for God's house suggests all that we're looking for and all that we need. It's the intimacy of being at home with God that gives us purpose and inspires us with a sense of direction through life. Every created reality has the potential to help us grow in friendship with God. Therefore, in our day-to-day living we are required to be impartial in our choices, asking ourselves if the choices we're making serve our goal in life. If they do, we embrace them, if not we surrender them.

In a sense, it doesn't really matter all that much what position in life we find ourselves in. We can praise God from our hospital bed to the same extent that we can when working hard in a busy airport. There are no limits to the times and places we can welcome God. The world is our oyster, providing a multiplicity of possibilities. We can embrace God as a poor person or as a wealthy person or as any other kind of person. So, if our goal is to welcome God, as Ignatius teaches, we get on with life, making the best decisions possible to implement that objective, wherever we find ourselves, and employing the unique distinctive personality traits we have inherited and developed. We don't have to be any other way than we are to praise God. It was Gerard Manley Hopkins, the Jesuit poet, who wrote: 'To lift up the hands in prayer gives God glory, but a man with a dung fork in his hand, a woman with a slop pail, give God glory too.'[11] Our contact point with God includes all our human experiences. Ignatian spirituality is unlike the more traditional spirituality with its emphasis on separating ourselves from ordinary and life-enriching human experiences such as marriage. For Ignatius, if our priorities are in order, and our hearts are in the right place, we will choose what we believe best serves the Ignatian goal of welcoming God into our lives.

It is given to us all to be able to honour God in a way that's unique and appropriate to us, by being who we are, which is a gift of God. Our role is to let our light shine and not hide it under a bowl. Many people can sing the same song, each with their own distinctive timbre – a tone that no one else can imitate. We acknowledge God's goodness by our 'selving'. This idea is expressed by Hopkins, who, it seems, invented the verb 'to selve', the process of maturing into our own unique individuality as our way of praising God. When we own our specific individuality, our purpose in life, everything else falls into place. We attain an increasing freedom from what distracts us from our purpose in order to be free for our purpose. However, this is the project of a lifetime with many twists and turns on the road.

This process is well illustrated early on in Sally Rooney's novel *Normal People*, when the teenage Connell is attempting to come to grips with who exactly he is. 'Lately he's consumed by a sense that he is in fact two separate people, and soon he will have to choose which person to be on a full-time basis, and leave the other person behind.'[12] Connell acknowledges to himself that he needs to start finding answers to serious

11   *Gerard Manley Hopkins*, Catherine Philips (ed.), Oxford: Oxford University Press, 1986.
12   Sally Rooney, *Normal People*, London: Faber & Faber, 2019, 26.

personal questions because his current life is failing to confront 'the ultimate question of what to do with himself or what kind of person he is'.[13] This kind of challenging reflection lies at the heart of the 'Principle and Foundation'.

Ignatius's 'Principle and Foundation' also develops the 'What's it all about?' question, posed by our novice human beings, by implicitly reminding us that it's about cultivating our true self as opposed to our false self. Our true self is experienced when we follow the path to what's good and God-like. The famous Cistercian monk, Thomas Merton, remarked that 'the problem of sanctity and salvation is in fact the problem of finding out who I am and discovering my true self.'[14] My true self is expressed through those experiences that facilitate my friendship with God, my relationship with myself, others and all created reality. My true self is my spiritual centre where I am who I am meant to be. This is summed up in St Catherine of Siena's words when she writes: 'Be who God meant you to be, and you will set the world on fire!' This reference to Catherine was in the opening sentence of the Bishop of London's sermon at the wedding of Prince William and Kate Middleton. He developed this idea by saying that: 'God meant each one to be, their deepest and truest selves.' Canadian poet Oriah Mountain Dreamer, in her poem 'The Invitation', captures the essence of this challenge when she says: 'It doesn't interest me / what you do for a living. / I want to know / what you ache for / and if you dare to dream / of meeting your heart's longing.'[15]

If my life is a matter of following the leader and trying to be like everybody else, I won't have lived. Who I am is not determined by others, by the celebrity or consumer culture. I am not what I have. I am not what I own. I am richer than that. But my false self would have me believe that unless I conform to the unquestioned cultural notions of success, I am a nobody. How sad is that mistaken idea! The fashion

13 Ibid., 28.
14 Thomas Merton, *New Seeds of Contemplation*, New York, NY: Dell Publishing, 1949.
15 Oriah Mountain Dreamer, *The Call: Discovering Why You are Here*, London: HarperCollins, 2003.

and cosmetic industries know only too well how to exploit our fears of failing to conform to the images of the body beautiful. There is no physically perfect person. A stroll on the beach in summer confirms this. Ignatius's 'Principle and Foundation' is a challenge to get beyond the script of the false self in all its shallowness.

The image of a jigsaw puzzle helps to develop a little more the idea of what life is about. Each individual piece plays an invaluable role. There are no substitutes. There is no understudy to replace me in life. We collaborate as co-creators with God by 'selving', owning who we are, and in that way we facilitate the completion of the jigsaw with our own unique contribution, as God had hoped for. It's only when all the pieces come together that the New Jerusalem, the new order of creation, will be established. While the kingdom of God is in our midst, it's awaiting its completion. We're not passive recipients in God's eyes. God needs each one of us to play the part assigned to us, by being who we are, faithful to our true selves. That's why it's so important to get in touch with what really makes us tick.

The story of how Richard Malloy SJ found his vocation is recounted in his book *Spiritual Direction – A Beginner's Guide*. It highlights the dynamics of the 'Principle and Foundation'. He describes how as a college student he enjoyed alcohol, the wild partying and the other attractions of student life until one night he had a fall that put him in hospital with a head injury. That was the beginning of a turning point in his life. Up to that time his life had been characterised by what Ignatius calls desolation, a feature of which is turning inwards while driven by the pleasure principle. Self-gratification, expressed in this case through the wild partying, is the norm. He describes how on his release from hospital he looked up at the moon and said, 'OK, God. If you're there, do something.' The realisation had begun to set in that he had lost his way in life and the pleasure principle was not hitting the spot in terms of meaning and purpose.

Coincidentally, that summer he got a job as an orderly in a care centre for the elderly which involved a lot of hard work, including bathing the patients, changing nappies and being at people's bedsides as they lay dying. He was surprised at how much he enjoyed the work. He was experiencing what Ignatius calls consolation, a feature of which is reaching out to others inspired by generosity. It's the opposite of the desolation already described. His elderly charges warmed to him and this made him wonder 'What is life all about? Why am I here? What am I going to do with my life?' Unknown to himself at that time he was engaging with the 'Principle and Foundation' and making good progress. His service to the elderly gave him a purpose in life he didn't have before by providing him with meaningful work. As a consequence of discovering what was important to him, and realising that serving others was so satisfying, he continued to mull over the question of what life was about. Gradually, over a period of time, he began to realise that he wanted to live a life of service following in the footsteps of Jesus. He eventually knocked at the door of the Jesuits to be admitted for training. He had come home to his true self.

A similar pattern can be seen in our search for the person who's going to be the lifelong partner. We may have experienced relationships that we initially thought were going to be the path of the future. As time progressed we realised that these relationships were not to be, for a variety of reasons. There was something missing – somehow they were disconnected from the fullness of the heart's longing. When the gut and the heart met, there was dissonance. Then we meet another, and find that there is a mutual echo in the heart that draws us together, and is expressed through reciprocal responsibility and respect. This is the moment we've been waiting for!

Many young people have participated in the Quo Vadis Pilgrimage Retreat, a three-day hike for final-year secondary-school students. Its theme is: 'Where am I coming from? Where am I now? Where am I going to?' The trek through challenging mountainous terrain mirrors the inner trek of dealing with these questions over a three-day

period. It includes a conversation with Cistercian monks at Mount
Melleray Abbey in County Waterford. On one occasion a monk began
the conversation by saying: 'If there is no God, I would not be here!'
This statement answers the first question. I come from God through
the unique circumstances of my life. The theme of the retreat echoes
Ignatius's 'Principle and Foundation'. Group and personal exercises along
the way facilitate personal reflection and affirmation. On one occasion
a student was heard to exclaim at the end of the retreat: 'This retreat
makes me want to go out there and do something with my life!' This was
his Cardoner moment, the eureka moment, when a person is willing to
meet the heart's longing. Ignatius would applaud the passion of this
kind of response. The 'Principle and Foundation' therefore is Ignatius's
tool for asking probing questions that penetrate the superficial layers
of life and challenge the script of the false self. Ignatius's fundamental
reflection helps us to focus on what life is really about once we get
beyond the trivial and superficial.

The Irish countryside is blessed with a variety of pilgrim paths.
Each pilgrimage has its own rituals and customs. Many pilgrims set
off with a clear purpose in mind, while others are not sure why they
have set out, much like the pilgrims who take on the challenge of the
Camino to Santiago de Compostela in Spain. In his 'Principle and
Foundation' Ignatius challenges us to get in touch with our core values,
what we really desire in our heart of hearts, as we make our personal
life pilgrimage. What happens between womb and tomb is of utmost
significance as we get only one shot at life – one opportunity to leave
our mark, to add to the store of the world's goodness, like the way we
pile one stone upon another.

Of course, there will be obstacles along the path. If we're lucky
we'll have only a few scrapes and bruises, the odd insect bite and a
bit of sunburn. Or maybe the worst thing to happen will be getting
drenched or we'll have to wait out a squall. But if we're unlucky we may
lose our way when the sea mist comes rolling in from the Atlantic and

obscures our navigation aids, such as a forest here and a stone wall there. Ignatius knew human life inside out. He was only too familiar with the inner landscape of the soul. He knew all about moods and feelings. He knew only too well what it was like to go around in circles in unfamiliar territory when the storm clouds gathered and when the thick fog descended. He had to spend long hours and days living in his own dark and desolate psychological deserts, bearing the brunt of the assaults of his own terrifying demons. He descended metaphorically into hell, especially when he wanted to take his own life due to the awful intensity of his darkest feelings which had got the better of him.

Thankfully, he was rescued by eventually heeding the sound advice of a Dominican friar, and he was helped to find the light that led to his true self where the quiet, gentle and compassionate voice of God drew him in the right direction. Life is like our sixth-year pilgrimage, with its ups and downs, its highs and lows. But others have travelled the terrain before us, leaving as their legacy a 'how to' manual to guide us when times are tough. Ignatius's series of reflections presents some of his insights to help us on our way. His guidelines help us to celebrate when things go well along the route. They also challenge us to deal with the times we get distracted and lose hope, experience discouragement and fall into a rut. They teach us how to retrace our steps. He helps us to put the zest back into life when monotony and routine leave us apathetic and listless, when we lose faith in ourselves and our potential. His wisdom helps us to make decisions that will kick-start and sustain the strategies required to be our true selves as an expression of our praise, reverence and service of God and others. We travel with so many others along the path of life, guided by Ignatius and his closest companion, who called himself Jesus, the Way. What better pilgrim companions could we have?

The challenge for all of us is to adapt Ignatius's 'Principle and Foundation' to our own faith and life situation. There are five helpful questions.

1. Where have I come from?
2. Who am I?
3. Where am I going?
4. How do I get there?
5. What do I really want along the way?

The summary chart that follows has the five questions on the left-hand side, and Ignatius's answers on the right-hand side, except for the final one which is more personal. It could be helpful to spend a little time meditating on these five questions and answers as a mini-retreat over a few days.

WHERE HAVE I COME FROM?	I come from God, through the circumstances of my birth, because God wants to share life and love with me and invites me into a friendship that never ends.
WHO AM I?	I am a person in whom God takes pride because I am. I am also the image of God. I am a person-in-relationship to God, the human family and all creation.
WHERE AM I GOING?	I'm on the way to the house of God in the company of others, to take my place at God's banquet, with all those who have gone before me.
HOW DO I GET THERE?	I get there by 'selving', becoming who I am, and using my talents in the service of my fellow travellers. I'm in solidarity, not competition, with my companions along the way.
WHAT DO I REALLY WANT ON THE WAY? (The answer tells me more about who I am and reveals my true self.)	I am enthusiastic about … What's important to me is … What gives me energy is … What really drives me is …

GOOD WOLF – BAD WOLF – WHICH IS WHICH?

In this chapter we will learn some more traditional Ignatian lingo. To help us stay on the right track in pursuit of the goal expressed in his 'Principle and Foundation', Ignatius includes twenty-two rules or guidelines in his Spiritual Exercises for what's called the 'discernment of spirits', which inspire either spiritual consolation or spiritual desolation. Discernment is a technical term for interpreting our conflicting feelings. In Ignatius's world view, two kinds of spirit exist. There is the good spirit who has our best interests at heart. There is the bad spirit, otherwise called the enemy of our human nature, who is out to undermine our peace. These 'spirits' are forces or energies for good and evil, which compete with one another in the heart of every person, just as in the Cherokee chief's story about the two wolves.

These forces leading to positive or negative outcomes are expressed through feelings, thoughts and desires, which help shape our moods. In order to know which feelings are good for us and which are bad for us, Ignatius has shared the wisdom of his experience to guide us. His guidelines are intended to help us reflect and distinguish between the different inner movements that we experience every day. While Ignatius understood these spirits in terms of his own sixteenth-century theological framework, we don't have to share his views to benefit from his insights. It's sufficient to see the person as fair game for either the good or the bad spirit. Ignatius helps us to identify which spirit is at work at any one time. We don't need to interpret the spirits as independent entities, inhabiting another zone, to benefit from Ignatius's wisdom. Such speculation is an irrelevant distraction from the core message. It's like focusing on the packaging rather than the content.

As a metaphorical way of understanding how we operate, the experience of countless people is that this model of spirits, good and bad, is immensely helpful. Ignatius didn't have a psychological vocabulary or access to contemporary models of understanding human behaviour, but it would be a pity to reject his presentation on the basis of such unfamiliar and historically conditioned imagery. Many of us prefer to access complex and abstract ideas through the gateways of visual imagery and narrative. The best teachers are those who can make concrete what is abstract and Ignatius succeeds in this.

Strictly speaking spiritual consolation and spiritual desolation are technical terms unrelated to our usual everyday meaning. They are, rather, related to our spiritual experience. Within Ignatian spirituality they have a very specific meaning as expressed in his guidelines. Both spiritual consolation and spiritual desolation arise within a specific faith context and a person's relationship with God. A person may pray every day and find that it makes them feel closer to God during their prayer time and during the course of the day. This experience is called spiritual consolation because the feelings and mindset are connected explicitly to a spiritual event – prayer.

Over time they may begin to experience an increasing lack of interest in prayer. It's not delivering the feel-good factor. They don't feel as positive about it as they did before. It feels as if God is distant or even absent. Discouragement and increasing half-heartedness take over. The person is inclined to take shortcuts where prayer is concerned or to give it up altogether. 'What's the point?' 'I can't think of anything else that could be so boring!' 'I could be catching up on those chores.' This is an experience of spiritual desolation because the feelings are directly linked to a specific spiritual exercise. The person's feelings are leading to them to give up on a good practice.

Alternatively, a prayerful person having a row with a friend brings the matter to God in prayer. Both parties in the row are equally stubborn. After a few days of prayer the person sees how silly it is and is drawn to take the first move, even though it's not easy. This is spiritual consolation, where a prayerful experience leads to reconciliation.

However, the good news is that the guidelines can be adapted and interpreted to suit other situations, such as getting a handle on how to deal with our fluctuating moods. The bottom line in interpreting 'spirits', feelings or moods is where they are leading. If they are serving our best interests, expressing our core values and making us less egotistical, and leading us to serve others, they're probably coming from God's Holy Spirit, whose energy we all partake of. But feelings can be so ambiguous! Ignatius has shared his guidelines to hone the art of discernment, asking questions such as: 'Where is this mood leading me?' 'What's driving this mood? Anger, resentment, contentment, generosity, self-giving or self-indulgence, discouragement or encouragement?' Competence in the art of discernment helps us to make good decisions consonant with our true self expressed through our core values. For Ignatius it's about paying attention to what's happening in our lives and interpreting our experiences with a view to action.

Ignatius did not welcome or allow everybody to do the full Spiritual Exercises until he felt they were psychologically and emotionally mature. He postponed the Exercises for a few years in the case of St Peter Faber, one of the co-founders of the Society of Jesus. Only when he had attained sufficient spiritual maturity did Ignatius allow him to begin. Peter Faber had a terrifying image of God and he had to wait until he had matured in that regard. As a general rule it could be argued that the guidelines on discernment are for those with an age-appropriate capacity for self-reflection.

The guidelines are no substitute for self-help where a diagnosis of a psychological problem has been made. The appropriate remedy for such disorders is within a clinical setting under the guidance of suitably qualified personnel. The characteristics of spiritual consolation and its opposite, desolation, may sometimes resemble symptoms of chronic depression, manic elation, hysteria, anxiety or other psychological disturbances. Distinguishing one from the other is the role of professionals. Discernment of spirits in an Ignatian context is the interpretation of the ordinary ebb and flow of emotions experienced by the average person going about their daily routine. Discernment, within the context of these reflections, is meant as an ordinary rule of thumb for the reflective person.

Ignatius believed, on the basis of his own experience, that when we go beyond all the outward appearances of our lives, and beyond all the various roles we play, we will discover our deepest desires, which coincide with God's hopes for us, in the way that parents have hopes for their child. This is understood as God's will for a person, as opposed to the false idea that God is the puppet master, pulling the strings in conformity with the script. This idea of God implies the absence of human freedom and portrays a God who's not possible to trust or believe in. In this understanding of God, my friend who gets knocked down by a car is playing out a pre-ordained role in conformity with God's script. What kind of absurd God is that? Yet, sadly, there are many who believe in such a God! Unfortunately, it's often the case that when a person says they do not believe in God, what they really mean is that they do not believe in misleading images of God that any sensible person would reject.

The novelty of Ignatius is that God speaks to us in the depths of our heart through our desires, thoughts and feelings. It's as if we are hardwired to be like God, but for all kinds of increasingly complex reasons the truth of our existence can evade us. What Ignatius calls disordered attachments can get the better of us – pride, greed, fear, perfectionism, the insatiable appetite for instant affirmation generated by social media, over-stimulation, the expectation of 24/7 availability, failure to realise we're stewards of creation and not its owner, obsession with prestige and status, the 'I have more than you' syndrome and all the other attractions that draw us away from God, ourselves and others, leaving us in a state of emotional turbulence, excitement and exhaustion.

My worth as a person is not determined by what I have. My material possessions, my academic attainments, my successes, my income and my bank balance do not define my worth as an invaluable and unique human person. My worth is not determined by what's outside myself. The bad spirit, the enemy of my human nature, would have me believe otherwise. I'm infinitely richer than that. It's so easy to get caught up in what we think we need and desire, but in the cold light of day we see the illusions for what they are. Solidarity with one another, rather than competition with one another, is God's idea of what life is about.

We can fail to realise that we share the same spiritual genetic make-up as Jesus, our pilgrim companion, which finds its true expression and happiness in choosing love over hatred, generosity over hoarding and self-sacrifice over self-indulgence, and all the other traditional gifts of the Holy Spirit that people of all faiths and none can easily agree on, as they are what fundamentally make us human and guide us into our true self. In the course of any one day our basic orientation may be positive. We may be in good space, going in the right direction, but there may be one area or more where we're struggling. It's a bit like a person whose basic health is perfect but who is suffering with toothache and a strained muscle. The aim, with the help of Ignatius's guidelines, is to get the whole body into shape, as countless people have done since the Spiritual Exercises found their way into the public domain. What Ignatius wants for us is the deep-down contentment that flows from our true self while living God's dream for us. No one ever said that life is going to be easy or, if they did, they were wrong! It's like training for the soccer or hurling final. It takes commitment, teamwork and a lot of self-sacrifice. But when a captain holds that cup up in the air on behalf of her team mates, we all know it was worth the effort, the blood, sweat and tears. In Ireland, we love to hear those words, drilled into us since our youth: 'A dhaoine uaisle, tá an-áthas orm an corn seo a ghlacadh ar son foireann' wherever it is. That's what Ignatius is getting at. I have the goal, now let's get going! What steps do I need to take?

MEETING THE WOLVES

In this chapter we will learn how to identify whether our moods are being influenced by the good or the bad spirit. The key words to keep in mind are: consolation, desolation, good space, bad space, good spirit and bad spirit. The Cherokee tale about the good wolf and the bad wolf competing with one another is a helpful metaphor for Ignatius's two spirits vying for our attention. What we feed the wolves is significant. If we feed the good wolf all the gifts of Ignatius's good spirit, we will live in a good space. In this case we will be guided along the path of encouragement, reaching out to others and nurturing all those other life-enriching qualities. Remember, it's what you feed the wolf that counts.

If, on the other hand, we feed the bad wolf with what Ignatius's bad spirit offers us, we grow into desolation, similar to bad space. In this case we will be guided along the path of discouragement and turn in on ourselves, feeding the bad wolf with self-pity, resentment, anger and other bad food, empowering the bad wolf to conquer the heart. We know what it's like not to let go of moods that are not good for us and how they can snowball.

The first and most fundamental question is: How do I know if I'm in consolation or desolation? The most important question for evaluating our moods is: Where are my desires, thoughts and feelings leading me?

Are they inspiring me to reach out to others or to turn in on myself? I'm in consolation if my orientation is towards others, and I'm in desolation if I'm turning in on myself. That's the basic rule.

The two spirits Ignatius speaks about are like two actors on the stage. Each spirit has a specific role to play. They know their script. Our mood is the cue. We too have a role to play. We're not passive, sitting around doing nothing. Ignatius tells us how to act when these two spirits are at work. The role of the spirits and our role are outlined in these fourteen points:

1. When we're in consolation, good space, the role of the good spirit is to affirm and encourage us. In this case the script of the good spirit will be coaxing me to stay on the right track. 'Well done. You're doing a great job. Keep it up!' My response is to savour the moment and enjoy the good times.

2. When we're in consolation the role of the bad spirit is to do the opposite, to sow doubt, discourage me, distract me from my path. The script will be negative. 'You'll never be able to last the course!' 'If people knew you were going on retreat, what would they think?' 'You'll make a fool of yourself!' 'You've never done that before, you're setting yourself up for a fall!' In that case, I'll recognise the tricks of the bad spirit, ignore the negative suggestions and think positively.

3. When we're in desolation, bad space, the role of the good spirit is gently to facilitate our return to the better path by giving us an encouraging nudge. If I'm in bad space, I'll feel healthy pangs of conscience when I listen to the script of the good spirit. 'You can do better than you're doing.' 'There's a lot more to you than you think.' 'Remember how well you managed before, don't give up now.' 'Why are you short-changing yourself and others?' 'You're giving in to a discouragement that will pass.' When I hear this script, I'll respond to the confidence the good spirit has in my

potential for growth by taking appropriate steps that I've already decided on when in good space.

4. When we're in desolation, bad space, the role of the bad spirit is to encourage and affirm us in the negative direction in which we're travelling. The bad spirit nurtures a devil-may-care attitude, facilitating needless cul-de-sacs, as in Richard Malloy's story. To get his own way, the bad spirit taunts us. 'You've tried to do better before, but you didn't make it, you made an utter fool of yourself. So, why bother? Stay as you are!' 'Listen, it's not worth the effort of trying to change. You know it's a waste of time.' My response is to take positive action. I won't give in to defeat.

5. To intensify the discouragement and loss of hope, the bad spirit will use the bullyboy tactics of unhealthy guilt, making the person feel so bad about themselves that they will find it difficult to escape from this dark prison. Ignatius was so immersed in these dark feelings that he contemplated taking his own life. It's essential to recall that God's work is gentle, that he has seen it all before, been there and done that. The agenda of the bad spirit is to keep us locked in despair, thinking there is no way out. This is a lie.

There is nothing to stop us reconnecting with God and others, no matter how bad we feel. There is light at the end of the tunnel, but our impaired judgement tells us otherwise. The bad spirit really rubs in this lie. And the bad spirit is not our friend. The bad spirit is our enemy who has our undoing in sight. Would we really trust an enemy?

Sadly, by giving in to these negative feelings, Ignatius made things worse for himself. But he learned from experience to reject the bad spirit. It's essential to be firm and robust in doing the opposite of what the bad spirit wants in this situation. Ignatius's confessor told him to stop repeating himself in confession. Following Ignatius's advice, I'll do the opposite of what my negative feelings tell me to do, and act as if I'm in good space. Rather than take to the bed or the drink or their equivalents and give in to my negative feelings, I'll do a kind deed for someone in need or simply give myself a break by finding something positive to distract me and restore my energy.

6. The role of the bad spirit, Ignatius also emphasises, is to get us to change serious decisions that were made when we were in good space. When we are in desolation, it's the bad spirit who's in the driving seat, so it's not the time to make significant decisions. Decisions made in bad space will come to naught. The middle of a sustained emotional storm is not the time to make a marriage proposal, or to quit our job or our marriage. How often we regret what we did and said in the heat of the moment! Words slip out that can never be unsaid. Deeds accompany us for the rest of our lives. Ignatius proposes a number of decision-making guidelines to help us make the best choices possible by paying close attention to our moods and discouraging us from making rash decisions (see Chapter 8). This will help you to avoid making decisions in bad space.

7. The role of the bad spirit is also to get us to be secretive and keep things to ourselves. If we have an issue that's bothering us, it will fester and will drag us down with worry. It will drain our energy and contribute to bad space unless we speak with someone we trust. A burden shared is a burden halved. Human beings all share similar problems. None of us invented anything in the problem or sin departments. As Fr Rossi de Gasperis SJ remarks: 'There is room for all the sins in the world, because God knows how to come back home.' Many of us are familiar with the bounce in our step

when we've been able to offload what's been bothering us to a confidant, to our medical practitioner or in confession to a priest. Our hope and trust are renewed. In the light of this advice, I won't bottle things up and will share where appropriate.

8. Consolation can have an affective dimension. In consolation I could have uplifting feelings that sustain me while going down the right path. But I can be in consolation without the emotional buzz. Enjoy the feelings while they last. They fuel energy and enthusiasm.

9. On the other hand, during a period of consolation, I could feel ill at ease, but my deep-down convictions give me confidence and affirm that what I'm doing is right. I'm facing a school test that's going to be challenging. I'm nervous about it. However, I'm not overwhelmed by anxiety. I know I've worked hard. My teachers have affirmed and encouraged me. So, deep down, I'm feeling confident. Even though there is a feeling of anxiety, it's the deep-down confidence that matters. This is consolation leading the person to take on a challenge with a degree of peace and calm.

I may be a shy person who has been asked to take part in the school show. My instinctive reaction is paralysing fear. I'm very uncomfortable. However, I think about it for a few days. I conclude that I'll give it a go. The fear doesn't go away, but I know in my heart of hearts that I can do it. My music teacher has often remarked on my singing voice. I'm willing to take the chance. This sounds like consolation, where the deeper conviction is more important than the surface feelings. In this scenario, I'll enjoy the satisfaction that comes from courage and conviction. I'll take pride in my achievements and be grateful for my talents.

10. In desolation, a common feeling is discouragement coming from my failure to live up to my ideals. 'I've failed again. Why bother?' When this happens, I'll acknowledge my discouragement and move on as best I can in the knowledge that it will pass and that giving in to negative feelings will only encourage them and make things worse.

11. In desolation, I could have great feelings, without a care in the world, as I continue to wander further and further from my true self, oblivious to the consequences for myself or others. I'm becoming more and more irresponsible in my dealings with others and myself and I'm not bothered. If I can recognise this with the help of the good spirit, it's a wake-up call to review my priorities.

12. Ignatius is realistic when he tells us that we can sometimes expect consolation, and sometimes desolation – times when our enthusiasm and energy can be drained. That's a fact of life. He advises us that when we're in good space we should find strategies that will help us through the bad moods so that they don't feed on themselves and get worse. Feeding the bad moods is like feeding the bad wolf until it gets bloated enough to squeeze out the good wolf. If we can identify the triggers that lead us into bad space, we can put a robust tactic in place to reduce their impact, but it's essential to be faithful to the tactic that works. Having methods to deal with bad space will also help us to remain faithful to our commitments when the novelty has worn off or when they have lost their glitter. Doing our homework in this regard will pay off.

A particular student, teacher or work colleague may have the potential to push all the wrong buttons. Certain situations may trigger negative emotions. If we can identify the situations in advance, we can have our battle plan ready.

I will respond to Ignatius's advice by preparing strategies for dealing with the different kinds of bad space. I'll have a plan of action for moods that drain my enthusiasm. This homework is essential for my well-being.

13. Ignatius points out to us that not all consolation comes from the good spirit. It can sometimes be like a wolf in sheep's clothing. The bad spirit knows how to take advantage of our good points. If we're particularly conscientious and generous, the bad spirit is able to make hay while the sun shines. He may encourage us to volunteer for everything in sight, which, in turn, can minimise our commitment to our primary responsibilities. Before we know it, we're worn out from chasing our tail and finding that we lack energy for our real priorities. A highly respected Jesuit, now deceased, used to refer to this in his own inimitable way as 'eejity zeal!' Being aware of this reality can help us avoid situations that we'll later regret.

Those with a fragile and sensitive make-up need to pay attention to this tactic. We can't be everywhere at the same time. We can't serve everybody's needs all the time. We can't visit our mum in the nursing home every day when we have babies to look after. So many feel guilty because they feel they should be doing more than they are able for. This is the enemy at work, in sheep's clothing, taking advantage of a good, sensitive and caring person. It's easier said than done, but finding the right balance in the storm of life's challenges is essential. Sometimes self-care comes first. If our energy becomes depleted, or if we experience burn-out, then our desire to care for others will become frustrated while we recuperate. We may be forced by circumstances to do less rather than more. Therefore, I'll identify my strengths with a view to how they can be manipulated by the bad spirit.

14. On the other hand, the bad spirit can exploit our vulnerabilities to his own advantage. If we're prone to discouragement, anxiety, loneliness, fear, easily feeling down or other debilitating emotions, we may be tempted to self-medicate and end up in situations that we would rather not have got into in the first place, or do exactly what Ignatius warns against – reverse a good decision. Unfortunately, seeking inappropriate people, places and experiences or unsuitable activities to relieve our pain can leave us worse off than when we started out. This is a common mistake. We're well motivated. We want to get rid of pain but we're looking in the wrong places. Ignatius advises us to reject a turn on the road that is going to lead us astray. This is the classical Ignatian *agere contra,* which means doing the opposite of what we're tempted to do for the good of our own well-being. In this situation, I'll identify my vulnerabilities and how to tame them in order to prevent my wandering away from my true self.

One final observation on discernment needs to be made and a technical word explained. Those who know a little about the Jesuits may have heard the Latin word '*magis*', meaning 'more'. Anyone who has ever crossed the threshold of a Jesuit institution will have noticed the abbreviation of the Latin motto, AMDG, which means 'for the greater glory of God'. This motto and *magis* sum up the passionate commitment of Ignatius to his service of God. The recurrent theme in all his writings is wholehearted commitment expressed through the regular use of words such as 'more', 'greater' and 'better'.

However, the concept of *magis* can often be misunderstood and, as a consequence, generous people take on too much and undermine their primary responsibilities. This is not what Ignatius had in mind. In many instances the *magis* has become a kind of competition. 'I'm busier than you.' 'I'm doing more than you!' The *magis* doesn't focus on quantity but on quality. It focuses on the quality of my being and not on the quantity of my doing. Ignatius wants us to reflect on the quality of our commitment.

A married woman with four children under ten felt called to serve the needs of the homeless, seven nights a week after work, because she felt drawn to that, after reading the parable of the final judgement in Matthew's Gospel. A graduate of a Jesuit college, she had misunderstood the meaning of the *magis*. Intelligent and pragmatic discernment will dictate that the more generous and qualitative option is to spend the time with her family. The *magis* is really about the quality of my commitment in pursuit of my unique vocation in life. The *magis* is not the name of a game.

It's helpful to recall that wholehearted Ignatius writes to an aristocrat, Jerome Vines, that 'in work, even when it is of a religious nature, there should be moderation, to the end that one will be able to bear up under fatigue, which is impossible when work becomes excessive ... Let it be enough for us to do what we can ... I would even add this, that you ought to take more recreation than you do.'[16] The *magis* is about balance, good practical judgement, while honouring our primary irreversible commitments and taking into account our own circumstances. *Magis* will sometimes mean quantitatively less and sometimes more. It's a qualitative commitment that will take precedence over a quantitative commitment. While Ignatius emphasised *magis* he also learned that '[h]is generosity to do even greater things for God than Francis and Dominic was contaminated by a selfish competitiveness'.[17] *Magis* is best understood as wanting to be more, to give more out of love for God and others, not for any reasons of competitiveness.

An abbreviated and adapted account of some of the main principles of the 'Discernment of Spirits' can be summarised as follows:

---

16 William J. Young, *Letters of St Ignatius of Loyola – Selected and Translated*, Chicago, IL: Loyola University Press, 1959, 413–14.
17 George Aschenbrenner SJ, *Stretched for Greater Glory*, Chicago, IL: Loyola Press, 2004.

GOOD SPACE = GOOD SPIRIT		BAD SPACE = BAD SPIRIT	
GOOD SPIRIT	BAD SPIRIT	GOOD SPIRIT	BAD SPIRIT
Encourages	Discourages	Discourages what's not good	Encourages what's not good

NAMES FOR THE GOOD SPIRIT OUR FRIEND, GOOD WOLF MY TRUE SELF IS:	NAMES FOR THE BAD SPIRIT OUR ENEMY, BAD WOLF MY FALSE SELF IS:
Love	Selfishness
Joy	Sadness
Peace	Agitation
Patience	Impatience
Kindness	Unkindness
Generosity	Self-centredness
Faithfulness	Unfaithfulness
Gentleness	Coarseness, loudness, pushiness
Self-control	Self-indulgence
Calm	Turbulence
Considered decisions	Impulsive decisions
Response	Reaction
Truth	Untruth
Just	Unjustness
Hope	Despair

Trust	Cynicism
Optimism	Pessimism
Respectful	Disrespectfulness
Ordered life – focus and goals	Disordered life – going nowhere
Freedom for	Compulsive – addictive
Service of others	I come first – narcissistic
Community	Egoism – me centre stage
Humility	Inflated pride
Part of solution	Part of problem
Life enhancing	Life impoverishing
Integrity	Fragmentation
Goodness – God	Absent goodness – the enemy
Authenticity	Inauthenticity
Sense of humour	Rigidly serious
Perspective	Lack of perspective
Flexible	Rigid
Compromise	I did it my way
Grateful	Entitlement
Appreciative	Taking for granted
Affirming and encouraging	Begrudging and discouraging

Reading St Paul's hymn to love in his first letter to the Corinthians (1 Cor. 13) and his description of the gifts of the Holy Spirit in his letter to the Galatians (Gal. 5:22) will enhance these points and help us to assess where we are in the mood department.

IS GOD HERE?
FINDING MY WALKING
COMPANION

In this chapter, two new concepts are introduced. The first, 'finding God in all things', is a central idea of Ignatian spirituality. The second, the 'Examen of consciousness', is a prayerful reflection on the bread-and-butter experiences of daily life. This chapter explores the concept of 'finding God in all things', while Chapter 6 discusses the Examen.

Ignatius believed that God metaphorically speaks to each person through their feelings, thoughts, desires and activities. For prayer to be as beneficial as possible, a working knowledge of the discernment of spirits, as discussed in the previous chapter, is helpful. However, a word of caution is advised. The idea of 'finding God in all things' can be over-simplified. God is not some perky little poodle who performs tricks at our beck and call. God is God, who can never be completely understood (an unfathomable Mystery). God is also immanent, present with us through the fact of Jesus' humanity, particularly in the sacraments and other privileged locations, such as scripture, community and nature. In addition, God identifies Godself with each person, especially with those who are suffering. Just as we can never fully fathom another person, so we can never fully fathom God. Therefore, we need to be humble when talking about God and 'finding God in all things', which is why some basic knowledge of discernment is necessary.

Ignatius's greatest legacy is the challenge to open our eyes in search of the traces of God's presence outside the stereotypically conventional places we normally associate with religion. There is often a perception that God is confined to churches, religious services and 'holy' places, objects and persons, with 'holy' taking on a severely restricted, other-worldly meaning that excludes mere mortals. The idea of God's presence being everywhere is neatly summarised by the French author and broadcaster, Yves Boulvin: 'Tout n'est pas Dieu, mais tout parle de Dieu' (Everything is not God, but everything speaks of God).[18] We would really have something to celebrate at Sunday Mass if we adopted this attitude. Eucharist, thanksgiving, would take on another meaning. It would be more like a picnic in the park with much to celebrate. God speaks the language of love, the language that keeps us alive. Ignatius asks us to pay attention, to listen to where love is spoken.

Limerick-born author Tom Stack, in his book on the Irish poet Patrick Kavanagh, well known to countless numbers of Irish secondary-school students, remarks that Kavanagh 'had a special gift for investing the natural world with spiritual significance'.[19] This is as good a definition of 'finding God in all things' as any other.

Stack continues in the same vein, saying that Kavanagh, 'could turn apparently inconsequential items of every day into an experience of hope and delight ... he was graced with what might be called a sacramentalising talent.' He explains what's meant by sacrament when he says: 'In sacrament we divine God's presence in particular material entities, in events and relationships ... It is a sign from creation already existing.' Finding God in all things is the gift of a mindset that facilitates a mystical view of the world, seeing beyond appearances, giving the sense that we're on sacred ground, continually being breathed into life by a Presence whose love has the intensity of a blazing fire.

---

18 Yves Boulvain, *100 chemins pour découvrir Dieu dans la vie de tous les jours*, Nouvan-le-Fuzelier, France: Éditions des Béatitudes, 2013.
19 Tom Stack, *No Earthly Estate*, Dublin: Columba Press, 2004, 17.

Kavanagh encapsulates this sense of mysticism when he writes in 'Street Corner Christ': 'I saw Christ today / At a street corner stand, / In the rags of a beggar he stood / He held ballads in his hand / And I whom men call fool, / His ballads bought, / From Him whom the pieties / Have vainly sought.'[20]

It's a wonderful poem, reversing our expectations of where we might find God and challenging us to open our eyes, to see things in a new way, in this case intuiting God's presence in the marginalised and vulnerable.

North American poet Sylvia Plath, in her beautiful poem 'Black Rook in Rainy Weather', writes about poetic inspiration, suggesting that it's how we see things that matters, in the same way that Ignatius's religious experience on the river bank in Manresa changed his whole perception of reality and gave him the encouragement he needed. Finding God in all things is a way of penetrating the reality of experience, which is richer than we imagine. What a tragedy to walk through life blindfolded!

On a cautionary note, we should remember that when we are in the middle of an experience we may not be aware of its total significance, such as when a family member or friend dies suddenly and we're plunged into a dark abyss of despair, our thoughts and feelings all over the place, hardly able to function. We're shocked and numbed. We don't know how we feel or what to think. The bottom has fallen out of our world. A person was once asked in such circumstances, 'Where are you finding God in this?'. It was the wrong question to ask at that time. In such a time – when it can feel as if God has also died in the process – we have to act with care .

Sometimes it's only after the event that the fragmented bits and pieces of life might fall into place and, with hindsight, a pattern may begin to emerge. The kindness of the people who brought meals and sandwiches to the house might be acknowledged as a sign of God's tender support. Or the sensitivity and the delicacy of the undertaker may

---

20   From *Patrick Kavanagh: The Complete Poems*, Peter Kavanagh (ed.), Newbridge: Goldsmith Press, 1988, 27.

be remarked on and again point to God's kindness. When we experience the adolescent 'growth spurt' we don't actually feel our limbs stretching one at a time. When we look back at old photos, or see ourselves in the mirror, we're amazed at what's happened to us without our noticing it! Where 'finding God in all things' is concerned patience and common sense are required. Let's not rush around impetuously assigning God our own pet categories, and, where possible, let's be humble enough not to rush to conclusions. Recall that consolation can pass itself off as a wolf in sheep's clothing. The fruit of finding God assumes that we will turn outwards rather than inwards.

How can we possibly 'find God in all things'? First of all, at Sunday Mass, we pray in Preface VI, just before the Eucharistic Prayer: 'For in you we live and move and have our being.' It's God's life and energy that sustain us. Therefore, that very fact of being sustained by God's energy is already a sign of God's presence in our lives. We already participate in God. If the sun were to burn out, there would be a cosmic catastrophe. If God were to burn out there would be hell to pay, because stretching the meaning of King Lear's words in the eponymous play by Shakespeare, 'Nothing will come of nothing.' Fortunately, we already tread on Holy Ground that awaits its transfiguration on the Last Day. We're already within sight of the Heavenly Jerusalem where the house of God is located and where its inhabitants wait to welcome us. When we die the energy that keeps us going now will be transformed by the power of the resurrection into an even higher voltage. It's in God that 'we live and move and have our being' for ever.

The list in the left-hand column at the end of Chapter 4 is a list of the gifts of the Holy Spirit as found in St Paul's letter to the Galatians, together with a number of other positive characteristics that St Paul could easily have added to his list. On the right-hand side of the list is the opposite of each positive word. Let's take love, for instance. God is the author of love, and the various ways in which it expresses itself feature on the list. In scripture we're reminded that 'God is love'. God cannot not love. God and God's loving cannot be separated. Love is God's identity. Love is God's name. Love is like a kind of blazing fire, similar to the sun, belonging to God, before which we sit in order to warm ourselves. We are guests before it, participating in its warmth, and sharing that warmth with others. 'Finding God in all things' is code, therefore, for identifying when and where we're drawn into experiences where we can say, 'God's action is here and therefore God's presence is here'. William Blake gets to the heart of the matter when he says in 'The Divine Image': 'Where Mercy, Love, and Pity dwell / There God is dwelling too'. This is an encouraging rule of thumb. When someone speaks an affirming and kind word to us, God is present, because that person is embodying God's affirmation and kindness. In a similar way, when a person sees more in us than we see in ourselves, and gently challenges us, God is present.

When we ask ourselves, during our daily Examen of consciousness, where and when we experienced love in its various guises during the day, we discover that we have found God and, vice versa, that God has found us. It's a bit like saying that God is the dancer and the dance is the gift. You can't have one without the other. The criterion for judging whether or not we have experienced God is the answer to the question: 'Where is this experience leading me?' If my 'finding God in all things' is leading me towards generosity and service of others, then I've found God and vice versa. This is where Ignatius's guidelines for the discernment of spirits play a critical role.

On the other hand, if my 'finding God' is not moving me to reach out to others in generosity and service, I may need to do further reflection, because I may be confusing 'finding God' with 'indulging myself'. This is somewhat evident in the way different spiritualities are 'marketed'. Some tend to be self-absorbing experiences promoting good feelings but directed inwards rather than outwards. While experiences that nourish the spirit are essential and to be welcomed, the distinguishing feature of Ignatian spirituality is its outward direction, expressing the true self in a way that's consistent with our spiritual DNA. Experience confirms that real happiness is to be found in giving expression to our natural orientation to be intelligently and prudently other-centred, consistent with Ignatian discernment guidelines. Expressing who we are, a person-in-relationship, is what leads to true happiness.

Returning to the funeral scenario, those who came to console and support that particular family by expressing their condolences were the concrete sign of God's presence. During the appalling Holocaust during the Second World War, people were devastated at the scale of the slaughter of men, women and children. For the victims it was a crisis of faith. 'Where was God in all of this?' However, as some have pointed out, while it is natural to empathise with the question arising from the depths of a wounded and broken heart, perhaps the more accurate question should have been: 'Where was the human person in all this?' It was estrangement from an authentic moral vision, on the part of human beings, that made the Holocaust possible. It was man's inhumanity to man played out in the desert of despair. Humans denied the God of compassion in the hope that what God stood for could be wiped out. It was a narcissistic humanity that temporarily eliminated God. However, God's compassion had the last word, incarnated or embodied in the compassion of those who took action to reverse the abomination. So, the point is that we find signs of God's presence in the good that we do to others and the good we receive from others. We are charged with God's energy when we have those experiences. If we're charged with God's very own energy, then God is present. The mysterious energy that keeps God going, keeps us going! That's how and where we find God in all things. The same applies to the other positive words on the list, which are different facets of faith, hope, charity and other life-enhancing characteristics from the good spirit.

When the news of Jean Vanier's sexual abuse of women came to light there was shock and disbelief. How could it be that such a man could have fallen from grace? The revelation of his actions served to reinforce our awareness of evil in the world. At that time Thomas Reese SJ wrote an excellent article in the *National Catholic Reporter*. He concluded by saying, 'Granted that we have been struggling to survive ever since we crawled out of the muck, evil does not surprise me. I am surprised by the problem of good. Why is there good in the world? Given where we came from and the world in which we live, why is there love? Why is there self-sacrifice? These are miracles of grace.'[21] A grace is a gift from God and, as we have already seen, the Giver and the gift are two sides of the one coin. Love in its various guises, including forgiveness, generosity, self-control, fidelity to promises and staying the course, are signs that we are on holy ground where God treads. Let's not take the miracles for granted. At the end of Georges Bernanos's novel, *The Diary of a Country Priest*, we are reminded that 'all is grace'. Ignatius wants us pay attention in order to identify the traces of grace, which are daily miracles that penetrate the evil of the world. The 'Principle and Foundation' highlights that we are invited by God, through our reaching beyond ourselves, to facilitate the transformation of the world by embodying God's vision of a civilisation of love and justice where God's presence is seen and felt.

21 *National Catholic Reporter*, 25 February 2020.

GATHERING NUGGETS
– LOOKING AT MY DAY

The Examen prayer takes about fifteen minutes but can be adapted to suit the circumstances. A regular Examen is recommended – how it would change the world if practised by everybody! In fact, the Jesuit delegates for education, after their 2017 international conference in Rio de Janeiro, published an action statement, in which they agreed to promote the Examen of Consciousness in each of the schools to help students listen to their inner voice and learn the path of interiority.

Societal changes occur when we change on the inside. Just as happiness is an inside job, so also is societal change an inside job. In one of his morning homilies, Pope Francis remarked that the 'peace of the people is sown in the heart'.[22] What he meant was that what's on the inside spills over to the outside.

The first step, like starting any other prayer session, is to calm down and be still in the presence of God or whoever God is for us. It's a golden opportunity to step off the carousel for a few minutes to reflect on what matters. It also presents a chance to consider work-life balance issues. It's like taking a breather for a few seconds when climbing a mountain. It's drawing breath for the hard slog of the next stage. If we don't draw breath, we won't make it to the top!

22   Casa Marta, 9 January 2020.

There is a consensus among those who pray on a regular basis, that the busier we are, the more we need to pray. It's in prayer that perspective is restored. The same principle applies to busy people who don't pray. They need to find a way of taking a reflective break to refocus. The Examen is an ideal way to do this. Like everything else Ignatian it can be adapted to suit a person's individual or family circumstances. Losing perspective causes so many problems that any chance to refocus needs to be welcomed.

I begin by spending a brief period calming down. I can make a gesture that reinforces that this activity is different from my other activities. I might bow for a few seconds to acknowledge that I am now in a special space, acknowledging that I am part of Someone bigger than myself, while briefly repeating a mantra before taking up my position. The mantra can be a phrase from scripture or anything else that helps to focus the attention. Some may light a candle or focus on a small icon or family photograph, a special pebble or anything else that helps. While I still myself, I become aware of being a praying person, rather than that person with so many other roles. I then ask God to send the Spirit of light to help me to see and hear what God wants me to see and hear. Ignatius's insight was that God metaphorically speaks through our life experience, so we get into a listening mode with the tools Ignatius gave to help us. When I've stilled myself and asked God to shed light on my life, I move to stage two.

For Ignatius it wasn't money that was the root of all evil but ingratitude. In the Spiritual Exercises, in his wonderfully rich 'Contemplation for Attaining Divine Love', he asks the person doing the exercises to 'recall all the good things I have had from creation'. The key idea is that God is the giver of everything I have. It's similar to St Paul's idea in his first letter to the Corinthians (1 Cor. 4:7): 'Name something you have not received.' The second stage of the Examen is to recall what I'm grateful for. It's best to be precise and focus on actual realities rather than vague general ideas. It could be gratitude for getting that job or for baby's first steps. What a miracle that is! This section of the Examen may sometimes overlap a little with the third stage.

However, gratitude may not always be spontaneous or easy for some people. We live in a wounded world where we get caught up in the crossfire of the good, the bad and the ugly. Some of us are victims of natural disasters where we can lose everything. Others are victims of human exploitation in its multiple guises. Some are born into socio-economically disadvantaged conditions that minimise opportunities for a decent quality of life, where life can be a short, nasty and brutish daily struggle for survival. Others are born with special physical or psychological needs, which are a huge challenge to themselves and their families. Others are in so much psychological pain that they do not want to live. Some succumb to an illness that undermines the quality of life. The list goes on, and that's the reality.

How is it possible to be grateful when I have been dealt such a rotten card? Surely the response is to shake my fists at the heavens and curse God at the top of my voice? I wouldn't be the first to do it! There's a strong biblical precedent! It's a bit like being asked in the middle of the funeral when grief is palpable: 'Where is God in all this?' Jesuit theologian Karl Rahner expresses his perplexity at what can sometimes seem like God's silence in the face of suffering when he prays: 'Why are You so silent? Why do you enjoin me to speak with You, when you don't pay any attention to me?' These sentiments echo the painful and confused feelings expressed so poignantly in the Psalms of Lamentation.

In his poem 'The Wrong Beds', Roger McGough humorously illustrates life's perplexities: 'Life is a hospital ward, and the beds we are put in / are the ones we don't want to be in. / We'd get better sooner if put over by the window. / Or by the radiator, one could suffer easier there.' He continues by saying: 'Anywhere but here. We take our medicine daily, / not politely, and grumble occasionally.' And this leads to the insightful final line: 'We didn't make our beds, but we lie in them'.[23]

23   Roger McGough, *Collected Poems*, London: Penguin Books, 2004.

What wonderful metaphorical imagery to capture the essence of the human condition!

The question of suffering is outside the scope of these reflections. It is mentioned as a caution against being naive in the same way as it's easy to be naive in regard to the idea of 'finding God in all things'. Gratitude is a challenge for many. While there may be much in difficult situations to be grateful for, it can take time and patience, along with sensitive and caring support, to get to that point of gratitude.

Without trying to trivialise the enormous challenges that some people face, it is worth mentioning that it seems to be the case that the more gratitude a person experiences the more content they are. It is worth remembering that gratitude also needs to be prayed for so that we may get a glimpse of what God is doing in our lives, as difficult as that may be in adverse circumstances. If we look carefully, we'll be surprised by how blessed our lives are. William Wordsworth highlights this when he writes: 'That best portion of a good man's life; His little, nameless, unremembered acts of kindness and of love.' However, we don't always welcome God's blessings with an open heart. At the time a blessing may feel more like a thorn in the side. It's only afterwards that we come to appreciate it. It's a bit like having minor surgery. It's inconvenient and unwelcome at the time. But when we have recovered, we appreciate what we've been through.

A lack of ability to identify what we can be grateful for on a daily basis can suggest unrealistic expectations. Failure to be grateful is often associated with a grandiose sense of entitlement and the fallacious idea that 'I'm a self-made man or woman'. A sense of entitlement is a tragedy because it means that we are failing to acknowledge the truth of existence. If I'm not grateful, I'm living in a bubble of my own making, in the false belief that each man and woman is a self-supporting island. Whether we like it or not, every person is a person-in-relationship, to others, to the planet and to God. It's this set of relationships that makes me who I am. Gratitude to God and to others is the expression of that fundamental and intrinsic reality.

One of the reasons for societal breakdown appearing in so many forms is the failure to embrace the fundamental fact of life that we are each of us a person-in-relationship. The whole Brexit campaign and the increasing number of xenophobia-fuelled nationalistic movements ignore this view of the human person. When persons and societies become narcissistic, the threads that keep civilisation together unravel. A 'culture of selfishness and individualism is not what builds up and leads to a more habitable world: it is the culture of solidarity that does so, seeing others not as rivals or statistics, but brothers and sisters'.[24] In an age where building walls to exclude others is becoming the norm, Robert Frost's poem, 'Mending Wall', read at John F. Kennedy's inauguration, is an ironic reminder of the growing culture of exclusion. The antidote to narcissism and a culture of exclusion is gratitude, which is at the heart of Ignatius's spirituality. Imagine if narcissistic world leaders and others put time aside for a quality daily Examen, with a special stress on gratitude and its implications!

It's also worth reminding ourselves that perhaps it's only in a place of consolation, good space, when the good spirit is counselling us, that we may become aware of what it is we can be really grateful for. However, believing that a person can be a self-made man or woman can lead to desolation because such a belief denies a person's identity. If I don't know who I am, I don't know who my family is, and consequently I become disconnected and estranged from the human family. I end up abandoned, wandering the moors, looking for my identity and prey to the big bad wolf whom I've been feeding with my desolate notions.

The narrative of Adam and Eve in the first book of the Bible is an extraordinarily perceptive take on how humans tick. We don't choose our parents or the location of our birth. Our birth is a given. It's a fact of life. We can't change it. It's the beginning of a series of givens that will follow us through life. Adam and Eve wanted to unravel themselves as

24 Pope Francis, World Youth Day, July 2013.

persons-in-relationship. They didn't want to feel as if they owed anything to anybody. There's got to be a better way, they thought to themselves; we can be the lord and lady of our own future and do it independently of that visitor, who comes strolling through the garden in the cool of the evening as if he were the Lord of the garden!

They weren't happy with what they had already been given, the purpose of which was to support relationships. 'We want' was their mantra. They were like two-year-olds who had discovered the words, 'No' and 'Mine!', or like the spoilsports in the school playground. Their rejection of their fundamental identity, persons-in-relationship, has continued throughout the centuries. The spoilsports in the playground mess things up for everybody else, because all the actions of a person-in-relationship have consequences for the rest of us. The response to the Covid-19 virus served to illustrate this global connectedness. If the same energy, galvanised by this virus, were also to be channelled into poverty, hunger, lack of drinking water and other global issues, what a different planet we would inhabit.

Ignatius traces how our riches, which include anything from how we look, to our athletic prowess, to our material possessions, to how popular we are, can lead to honours in the sense, among others, of enjoying the prestige that comes from success. But the problem is that we can end up with an exaggerated pride by forgetting where we came from and who supported us along the way. When my pride gives me an exaggerated and arrogant sense of entitlement, I reject my true identity as a person-in-relationship and turn inwards in an unhealthy way. The rejection of our identity wreaks havoc, as history has demonstrated. It not only destroys our relationship with the rest of the human race but also with our planet. As the story of Adam and Eve illustrates, self-centred pride is not the foundation of happiness.

The role of the new Adam is to put us back together again and lead us into our true self by leading us to the table of the Trinity, the model of all relationships. That's where we'll find, along with our sisters and brothers, what we're looking for. It's there that our hunger and thirst will be satisfied. It's there that we welcome the bread and the wine to sustain us on the way, and to lift us up us when our spirits weaken with the burdens that inevitably cross our path.

German theologian Meister Eckhart encourages us by saying that if 'the only prayer you ever say in your whole life is "thank you" that would suffice'. In desolation, bad space, that challenging landscape where we're trying to negotiate our way in the darkness through a fog, it is difficult to identify what we can be grateful for until the light shines. Ignatius reminds us to prepare ourselves to deal with such a situation beforehand during good space, in order to avoid the worst intensity of the darkness. We need to have our torches and our maps in our backpack because we never know what's around the next bend.

Let's take three scenarios to highlight the nuts and bolts of the Examen. There are two fictional characters, Mary and Aoife. Aoife comes into work one day in bad space, having had a frustrating start to the day, including a commute that delayed her getting to work. She also got caught in a torrential shower and she's drenched to the skin. On the interior she's like a bat out of hell and on the exterior just about in control of herself. Her colleague Mary does what she can to help her dry out. As the morning goes on Mary invites Aoife to the canteen for a coffee. Mary expresses a few encouraging words of support. Aoife begins to feel a little more relaxed and is drawn to being more positive during the rest of the day.

During her Examen before going to bed, she identifies Mary's kindness as one of the high points of the day. She's grateful to God for Mary and how her intervention helped her regain perspective. It also inspired her do the same for anyone else in a similar situation in the future. This has all the characteristics of the good spirit. This is consolation. It's feeding the good wolf and leads to a good mood, inspiring positive vibes. Mary was the instrument of God's compassion by her openness to the good spirit.

Now let's look at a similar situation. Aoife was up most of the night with a sick child. She has missed her bus and arrives at the office exhausted and in bad form. Her work colleague now happens to be Amy, who has the reputation of being rather insensitive and self-centred. Amy notices that Aoife is not herself and under pressure. Instead of having the friendly chat, she makes sarcastic comments, which Aoife finds deeply offensive. After a while Aoife starts giving back as good as she gets. It becomes a verbal duel, one outdoing the other with cruel remarks.

When Aoife is doing her Examen before going to bed, she identifies her rotten feelings at impulsively acting so out of character during the day. She recognises that God's presence in terms of exercising mutual respect was not in the office. Her own impetuous reaction didn't help, and her feeling of desolation just added fuel to the fire, drawing her into uncharacteristic behaviour that reflected her worst self. Compassion and mutual respect were sadly missing. God's absence was experienced. Aoife was drawn towards the worst in herself. Before concluding the Examen she asks God's forgiveness for her part in making matters worse. Having reviewed the situation from start to finish, she prepares for potential future clashes with the likes of Amy.

Ignatius reminds us that the enemy, like a military commander, identifies our vulnerabilities and exploits them. Aoife needs to remind herself how she's going to react when she's in a low mood. In good space, she has devised a strategy to cope when her buttons are pushed. The following day, it's Amy who's on duty with her. But today Aoife is proactive in putting her strategy into place. She doesn't find it easy, but it works, and she returns home feeling good about herself for having done the opposite of what her bruised feelings dictated. In her Examen, she has much to be grateful for.

Harry and Jane have been married for fifty years. One Monday morning Harry is rushed to hospital with a life-changing stroke from which he never fully recovers. He is left unable to walk or swallow. He is totally disoriented and remains in that state for the rest of his life. His wife Jane takes the bus from her home a few days a week to visit him in the care centre. The visits are extremely hard on her as she watches her once robust and independent husband reduced to such frailty and weakness. She often has to turn away from her husband so that he doesn't notice the tears trickling down her cheeks. She comes away from the visits feeling low and lonely but determined to return because she feels it is the right thing to do. This is Jane's way of continuing to honour her marriage vows of fifty years.

In her Examen, Jane thanks God for the gift of her husband and the good times they shared together. She acknowledges the pain she feels at her husband's debilitating illness and how difficult she finds the visits. There is no affective consolation. There is an emptiness in her heart. But her visits highlight her experience of consolation because in this challenging situation she is drawn out of herself to look after her husband as long as she is able to. If she were in desolation, she would give in to her feelings.

For busy parents, the Examen may simply be a time of gratitude: gratitude for their children and their own love for their children. Regardless of how they feel, they have to honour their parenting responsibilities, which is a demanding and challenging task. They cannot abdicate their responsibilities to give in to bad space. They need to be particularly sensitive to how they manage desolation, bad space, for the sake of their children's emotional and physical well-being. How often do parents step up to the plate for the sake of their children even when they're not feeling up to it? This is heroism at its best. This is the ultimate self-giving of the Gospel. Parents need to recognise that this is their pathway to God, acknowledging on a regular basis how their practical expression of love for their children teaches them the most important language of all – God's language of love. When children look confidently into the eyes of their parents, they are looking into the eyes of God.

During their Examen prayer, parents would do well just to gratefully acknowledge some of the many good turns that they have done for their children in the course of the day, from putting food on the table, to ferrying their children here, there and everywhere and keeping the Bank of Mum and Dad solvent! This is their way of expressing their true selves and giving expression to the heart's deepest longings – to share life and love. This constant stream of love reinforces their identity as person-in-relationship. It demands tough staying power. In the spirit of Meister Eckhart, they can simply say 'thank you' to God for their children and the gift of generosity they have received from him, which allows them to welcome their children as part of their family. What greater love is there than giving up life for others? At a retirement party for his mother, the youngest adult child remarked how he and his siblings got to where they were in life only through the daily sacrifices of their mother, for whom no sacrifice was too great. The children hadn't forgotten how their mother's life had made such a huge difference and were grateful for it.

As the babies grow up, each stage presents different and never-ending challenges, which sometimes demand the wisdom of Solomon and the patience of Job! A parent's vocation never ends. Adult children, with their partners and children, may need to return to the nest during transition moments in their lives. Sometimes teachers and others act 'in loco parentis', meaning that they legally take on the duties of a parent. In dealing with their children parents are acting 'in loco Dei,' in the place of God, facilitating the holistic development of their child. What a privilege and a responsibility!

At a Sunday Mass, the gospel reading was on how we should take up our cross daily to be a follower of Jesus. The church was full of families with young mums and dads and others, some of whom had remained unmarried to look after elderly relatives. The homilist reminded everyone of the need to be harder on themselves in looking for penitential opportunities! How much harder can parents be on themselves than getting up in the middle of the night to feed their babies? Parents live on challenging holy ground, where they metaphorically, and sometimes literally, wash feet all day following the example of Jesus. They hardly have a minute to call their own. How much more can they give? None of us needs to seek out penances – they barge into our lives uninvited in so many different ways. Given the unending nature of parents' commitments, during their Examen prayer, they could do well to consider ways to take time out to 'smell the roses', as parents also need time to themselves to nurture their relationship.

In summary, then, the Examen looks like this. There are five stages, which can be adapted to suit the person and circumstances. The process takes about fifteen minutes, more or less. The time allocated to each stage is not meant to be absolute. Flexibility is required to facilitate whatever works best. The Examen is an excellent and accessible prayer available to all in a manner adapted to their personal circumstances.

However, the more ideal scenario is also to incorporate into your lifestyle other types of regular prayer, either employing Ignatian methods or any other kinds of practice you find helpful. Prayer is allowing God a window of opportunity to let his comfort into our lives, similar to spending quality time with a partner or friend. As we get more acquainted with God, we don't need to prepare big speeches, but can simply be in his presence without making a fuss and searching for words. Like people who know one another well, God can read the map of our hearts and knows when and how to deal with what's going on.

Prayer also gives us the opportunity to bring before God our own worries and all the people, both living and dead, lodged in our hearts. Spending time with God helps us to experience life in a new way. It doesn't always mean spending long periods in meditation. For busy people it could simply be regular short, sharp bursts when travelling on the bus or train.

Even if we feel that not a lot is happening when we pray or we're finding it challenging, there's more going on than meets the eye. In her poem 'Prayer', Carol Ann Duffy captures the experience well when she writes: 'Some days, although we cannot pray, a prayer / utters itself.' Prayer isn't a test on which we're marked. What matters most is putting some time aside, to make space for God and ourselves to catch up. And if we're feeling bored during prayer, it's comforting to remember that God is enjoying our company and appreciative of the fact that we have put time aside.

It's like many other experiences in life. We may go regularly to visit a neighbour with dementia. Sometimes the visit is enjoyable and there is a flicker of recognition on the part of the other person. Our visits are not always a thrill a minute for us, but that's not the point. We're visiting for the sake of the other person for whom a lot more may be going on than we think. Our patient presence to the other can do wonders for both of us.

What follows is an image of what the Examen might look like for those starting this practice for the first time. It looks mechanical but the detailed structure is meant to be nothing more than a scaffold. As we get used to it, we can simply adapt it. Sometimes it may be more probing depending on our life circumstances, and at other times it may simply be a prayer of gratitude for what we have received from God. Flexibility is what's important. Ignatius wouldn't want us to get imprisoned by the structure. What's important is to focus on what's touching the heart. The kind of day or week I've had will draw me to the points I need to review. If I've had a rotten day where everything seemed to go pear-shaped, I will need to focus on that with God at my side. But getting into as good a space as possible is essential to regain perspective, so I may need to spend more time than usual at the first step.

STEP 1 *2 minutes*	'Be still and know I am God.' Pray for light so that I see and hear what God wants.
STEP 2 *2 minutes*	Thanks to the Giver of gifts for: 1.. 2.. 3..
STEP 3 *4 minutes*	What spoke to me of God? Traces of God's presence? Love, kindness, generosity, peace, patience, joy, self-control? What lifted my spirits? Where did that lead me?
STEP 4 *4 minutes*	Signs of God's absence? Apathy, lack of consideration, meanness, agitation, impatience, gloom, self-indulgence? What dampened my spirits? Where did that lead me?
STEP 5 *3 minutes*	Sorrow and renewal. Tomorrow … pitfalls to avoid? Forewarned is forearmed!

GOOD RIDDANCE

There is a lovely story, *The Hurt*, written by Teddi Doleski and beautifully illustrated by William Hart McNicholas SJ. It's about a little boy named Justin who fell out with his best friend because he called him a bad name: 'Justin, you are a pig-faced punk.' This hurt Justin. His feeling of hurt was like a big hard stone that started to get bigger and bigger in his room. He began to brood on the bad things that had happened to him. His father gave out to him for leaving mud on the floor. The more Justin thought about the bad things, the bigger The Hurt became, occupying more and more space in Justin's bedroom until a time came when Justin was afraid there would be no room to manoeuvre. He couldn't sleep any more because The Hurt was even taking up his bed space. He got really scared and did what Ignatius told us to do in his discernment guidelines. He told his Dad what was going on and how he had been hurt by Gabriel and his Dad's reprimand for letting mud into the house. He also began to think of good things that had happened. Slowly The Hurt began to decrease in size until it disappeared altogether.

For most of us there is something in our lives similar to The Hurt, which increasingly occupies inner space that would be better filled with something creative and positive. The more we indulge The Hurt and feed it, the more cumbersome and awkward it becomes, like carrying a heavy weight on our shoulders. Indulging The Hurt is like feeding the bad wolf. Indulgence promotes growth.

The Hurt can appear in a variety of guises, such as a particular recurrent habitual pattern of behaviour that we would do better to get rid of. It could be chronic impatience, the predictable sarcastic remark, compulsive buying, an unhealthy relationship with alcohol or other drugs, irresponsible relationships, cyber-bullying, explosive anger and other behaviours that hurt and undermine our true self and others.

In religious communities, as well as other places, it can also be a failure to take responsibility for communal chores in the expectation that others will do them. It can include lack of sensitivity to others and failure to respect boundaries. Some may replace community engagement with 'virtual' friends. A disproportionate amount of time spent on the laptop, TV and social media or anything else can replace the quiet space that sustains prayerful wonder. The reasons for such behaviour need to be flushed out because addictive behaviour can be symptomatic of desolation, where things of the spirit and our regular occupations have lost their taste, which, as Ignatius repeats, is a fact of life. Discouragement and lack of faith in ourselves and in our ministry can also be the root cause of energies channelled away from our primary focus. The same dynamics apply to marriage.

Pope Francis, in a retreat to bishops, remarked that desolation, what he called 'acedia', an old-fashioned word, 'appears as a paralysis, when one can no longer accept the rhythm of life. At other times it is the hyperactive pastor whose giddy goings and comings reveal an inability to ground himself in God and in his concrete circumstances.'[25] The temptation to give in to the 'far away hills are green' syndrome is always present in all walks of life. Anywhere else but where we are!

We forget that we bring the same person to the faraway hills! We also forget that change happens on the inside. We believe some vague 'elsewhere' is going to cure all our angst and we will be resentful and

25 Jean-Charles Nault OSB, *The Noonday Devil: Acedia – The Unnamed Evil of Our Times*, San Francisco, CA: Ignatius Press, 2015.

blame everybody else for our malaise until we find it. This is a lie coming from the bad spirit. Just as societal change is an inside job, so too is happiness, which, as Victor Frankl has pointed out in his books, has a lot to do with attitude. In the face of powerlessness, I can at least choose my attitude. The cynicism that replaces trust and hope is an offspring of the bad spirit. Ignatius would want it nipped in the bud because cynicism with its sister, sarcasm, disappointed hope, feeds on itself, leaving bitterness and nausea in our spirit. This toxic diet makes the bad wolf overweight while taking over the heart. The sarcastic cynic is in serious desolation.

Dutch spiritual writer Henri Nouwen remarked with great passion that many of us want to be anywhere but where we are. He stressed the need to be patient, which he defined as the capacity to live in the real world where we find ourselves. As an antidote to this spiritual wanderlust, Oriah Mountain Dreamer remarks in her book *The Call* that 'There is simply no place, no location or situation, that cannot be used to wake up to and live all of what and who you are, if you are willing to show up, to be present in the only place you have access to: here.'[26] There may be other places that are more in tune with our preferences but ultimately each place has its own 'challenges and gifts'.[27]

Routine and monotony are intrinsic to every life. When feeling swamped by monotony we need to find imaginative new ways forward. This is one of the areas where Ignatian reflection during the Examen may help reignite passion. When we feel the light has gone out in relationships, occupation or vocation it can be helpful to remind ourselves what the attraction was like in the first place. What drew me to this person? What experiences drew us closer? What were the high points? Where did the cracks begin to appear? In a similar way we can remind ourselves what motivated us to take up a particular occupation. What experiences strengthened our motivation? When and why did the cracks begin to appear? What can I do now to reignite the spark?

26   Oriah Mountain Dreamer, op. cit., 78.
27   Ibid., 80.

It's a fact of life that the lustre can fade, and it is in this new place that I begin again, having learned from life and having become less driven and more patient with myself and the world. The hope is that I will now be more comfortable with my reality without becoming apathetic or imprisoned by it. Perhaps I can recognise the opportunities it offers if I can let go of my myopia.

As staleness affects all relationships, occupations and walks of life, it's easy to get into a comfortable rut. Therefore, as Ignatius recommends, when in good space we visualise how to spice up routine and monotony by taking risks. If we are teachers, it is essential to reflect on our teaching style regularly with a view to revamping it and incorporating the best of contemporary insights. If we're still teaching the same way five or ten years into our career, we need to take stock and discover how we can ramp it up. If we're in ministry and thinking and doing what we did and thought five or ten years ago, we need serious personal renewal. The Ignatian paradigm for education is experience, reflection and action. This is a model that can be applied by anyone in any walk of life. Adapting the Cartesian slogan, '*Cogito ergo sum*' (I think, therefore I am), for Ignatius it would be 'I learn, therefore I am'.

Conscientious people, driven by what appears to them to be the best of intentions, with a desire to save the world and full of initial fervour, may wear themselves out with ambiguously motivated overwork. Ignatius warns us about this phenomenon. Sadly, some of my motivation may unconsciously come from pride, my inability to say 'no', or my need to be liked, inspired by the bad spirit, which may lead to the seriously debilitating conditions of premature burnout, fatigue or depression. Therefore, Ignatius advises us to reflect on our experience, assess our motivation and make balanced generous decisions.

If I feel I'm moving towards burnout, fatigue or depression, the Examen is an opportunity to recalibrate the compass to recover diminishing energies. If I feel that I'm burning the candle at both ends, I am, and I need to re-evaluate my priorities. In his book, *Finding the Still Point*, Gerald O'Mahony SJ makes a critical observation. He wisely remarks that for a person trying to cope with the ordinary daily struggles and moods of life, 'There is far more danger in straining than there is in slacking, since a person who eases off can easily reverse the process, whereas a person who strains too much may "snap" and take months to recover.'[28] Sadly this has been the experience of many. Ignatian discernment is critical here in finding the right balance. When in doubt, take the easy way out!

The Hurt reinforces that any negative that steals our space and needs to come under the microscope so that dark spaces can be penetrated by the light. The paralysis that can come from losing hope and giving in to despair needs to be addressed for the sake of our physical and mental health.

It's important to recall that Rome wasn't built in a day. Our brains get used to behaviour patterns and progress is one step at a time, but it does happen. We need to start thinking of how to deal with the fundamental issues first. Cognitive behavioural therapy will tell me I'm not a mind reader, so I can't say if my boss is questioning my competency unless she says so. Feelings are not reality and must be tested out in the real world. However, more often than not, feelings are not tested. Therefore, what I feel and perceive is reality. This needs to be continually challenged. My boss may think I'm the best thing since fried bread but isn't yet ready to say so! It's my own lack of confidence, lack of perspective or other issues that may be generating my fears and unease during department meetings.

Mind-reading is often the root of much misunderstanding. We attribute to others thoughts and motives they do not have. A teenage girl comes into school and one of her best friends ignores her. She's upset and angry, so much so that she visits the school counsellor to deal with the feelings of rejection. She blames her friend for upsetting her by ignoring her. Later in the day it transpires that her friend didn't have her

28   Gerald O'Mahony, *Finding The Still Point*, Guildford: Eagle, 1993, 62.

contact lenses in! If we could only get into a state of equilibrium and see reason rather than rashly jumping to conclusions!

Embarrassing confrontations at parent-teacher meetings could be avoided if parents did some fact-finding beforehand rather than jumping to conclusions. Every parent thinks that their child is the best in the world, but indulging that fantasy does no one any good, least of all the child. Many teachers have had the embarrassing experience of verbal assault. 'There's a personality clash between you and my son!' Then the parent is patiently and politely told that their son doesn't do the required homework and that his behaviour with all teachers is somewhat problematic.

In the Spiritual Exercises Ignatius warns against interpreting what people say and do in a negative way. He encourages us to be 'more inclined to put a good construction on another's statement than to fault it' (SE, 22). What a difference this approach would make in avoiding misunderstandings! Others don't always deliberately set out to annoy us, but our mistaken mind-reading usually confirms our opinion that they have.

It's essential to be patient and stop presuming that my thoughts and feelings reflect reality until there is evidence to the contrary. In this way The Hurt will decrease and my burdens will be lighter. While many people might find Ignatius's tactic helpful, it may not suit everybody. Some complex personal issues may be better served by appropriate professional expertise, especially when others reject the facts in favour of their own mistaken and thwarted perceptions.

Of course, the Examen could also be used to promote the cultivation of positive habits intentionally, outside the context of focusing on negative patterns. I could employ this strategy to build self-confidence, improve my self-image and start to overcome fears and anxieties that are holding me back from living my life to the full, as God intended. The bad spirit has a way of short-circuiting our lives by filling us with false humility, which can paralyse the use of our talents.

I may be a shy person, who finds meeting others difficult. I'd like to accompany people with special needs but I'm not sure if I'd be any good. Speaking in public may be a nightmare. I can't eat all the apple in one go, it's one bite at a time. Using this strategy, I could set myself small goals on which to focus in a realistic manner and counteract the bad spirit with Ignatius's *agere contra*, to do the opposite. I would gradually expose myself to the situation that causes fear or anxiety. I could apply to myself the wisdom of one of Susan Jeffers's book titles: *Feel the Fear and Do it Anyway*. Ignatian consolation sometimes involves feeling the fear, but acting anyway, because I'm convinced it's the right thing to do, even though my fear is inspiring me to run away. The more I resist my fear, the more confident I will become.

I could have a page in my notebook where I track the progress in relation to the habit I want to develop. This approach has one positive advantage. It highlights success, and success builds on success, while sowing the seeds of encouragement. I could pleasantly surprise myself! Sometimes such simple charts can be more helpful than keeping everything stored in the mind. I could bring the chart to my Examen prayer to count my blessings in the presence of God 'in whom I live and move and have my being'. Like all things Ignatian, reflection is the key to unlocking the energy I need to grasp whatever nettle needs grasping and to identify which spirit I am being moved by.

William Byron SJ suggests taking a daily sheet to monitor ourselves in nine different areas inspired by St Paul's list of the gifts of the Holy Spirit. He recommends a morning and evening exercise just like Ignatius. For a habit such as generosity, he poses a question for the morning exercise. 'What will I be today, a giver or a taker?' The evening exercise asks other questions. 'Was I petty, ungiving or unforgiving in any way today?' 'Did meanness enter the world through me?' 'Did I make anyone smile?' 'Did I listen generously?'[29] These prayerful exercises could easily be done on the bus or driving to and from work.

---

29   William Byron SJ, *Answers from Within: Spiritual Guidelines for Managing Setbacks in Work and Life*, John Wiley & Sons, 1998, 29.

Of course, the evening questions could also be part of or even replace the Examen of Consciousness prayer. The nine areas Byron highlights are: joy, peace, patience, kindness, generosity, faithfulness, gentleness and self-control. However, time, place and circumstances will dictate what we need to prioritise. We can add whatever we like to the list to help us make progress. We do these exercises not just for self-improvement but to align ourselves with God's values against the background of paying attention to the traces of his presence in our lives. Experience confirms that it's values like these promote the peace and joy that God wants for us.

When Justin was able to name the negativity in his life, gradually replacing it with naming the positive, The Hurt began to lose its power over him. We hope that we can do something similar by naming the things that hurt and finding a way forward to get rid of them. The reflection of the Examen, and the two methods described can help us to grow into our true selves, where we'll find ourselves touched by the peace of God.

TAMING THE EGO FOR
DECISION-MAKING

It's a July afternoon in Tenerife South airport and the flight from Shannon has just arrived. At the boarding gate are two queues, priority and non-priority, ready to board for Shannon. A passenger pushes her way to the top of the non-priority queue and then has a conversation with one of the ground handling agents. No one has any idea what the conversation is about but the outcome is clear. She, along with another woman and two children, jumps the queue. They are now at the top of the non-priority queue. A handling agent approaches this group of four and has a conversation, the outcome of which is an almighty row over cabin baggage. The original passenger, now hot-tempered and in full flow is furiously arguing with the handling agent. The result is that she has to pay a hefty amount to get her bag on board. And does she let everyone know about it?

You can easily imagine the scene. A hot-tempered woman with a sense of entitlement, whose anger has been kindled because she can't have her own way. 'I'll never fly Bargain Air again!' Her shouting was loud and clear.

'I'll never fly Bargain Air again!' That was her decision. This way of decision-making in the heat of the moment contradicts Ignatius's way of decision-making. Firstly, the person making the impulsive decision is not in the appropriate emotional space required by Ignatius. Secondly, there is no data-gathering. It's a spur of the moment reactive decision fuelled by negative emotions. Thirdly, there is no objectivity weighing up the pros and cons. Fourthly, the decision is inspired by revenge rather than constructive motivation. This person wants to punish Bargain Air for what she considers is unjust treatment. She pulled a fast one and was found out! It's 'an eye for an eye!' and 'I'll get you back!' And the irony is the service handling agents she was fighting with and who had to soak up her explosive anger were not even employees of Bargain Air! Her outburst, driven by her own giant ego, was so disrespectful of others. What I want, I get! Everything in this vignette is so un-Ignatian.

Ignatius's rules for decision-making are found in his Spiritual Exercises. Many people who do the exercises are trying to make the best vocational choices possible within a faith context. 'Will I marry and continue the family business?' or 'Will I leave home and become a monk?' The purpose of Ignatian decision-making is to facilitate a closer relationship with God in order to make the best decision possible, taking into account a person's strengths and any blind spots that could impede good decision-making. One of the purposes of the Spiritual Exercises was to 'rid oneself of all irregular attachments', in order to get a better personal perspective on life, empowering clear-headed and balanced decisions when unwanted pressures were removed.

It is important that the person is familiar with the discernment of spirits, especially as, in the second method of making a decision, sifting through the different interior movements is essential. In this area, the enemy of our human nature can come into our hearts disguised as an angel of light. The bad wolf can appear as a lamb. Like all things Ignatian, the principles underlying his decision- making process can be adapted to suit our own circumstances.

The dispositions which the person making the decision brings to the process are at least as important as the methods suggested by Ignatius. As far as Ignatius is concerned decisions are a means to an end. He expects decisions to be inspired by generosity and to be the consequence of serious deliberation. The dispositions are summed up as follows:

1. A person must be in the best possible state of equilibrium, the opposite to the woman in the airport. Ignatius uses a metaphor to describe this kind of solid personal space. He compares it to the scales you'd find in a chemistry lab. There are two small containers on either side. They must be balanced without a slight leaning to the left or to the right. For Ignatius it's important to wait for this kind of space if time allows. This state of equilibrium should be consolation in its broadest sense. The other side of this guideline is never ever to make decisions in bad space because, as we saw in his guidelines for discernment, it's the enemy of our human nature who's doing the driving. We know from experience that driving with the enemy only leads to disaster, something the woman in the airport will learn to her cost when she's paying higher fares with other airlines. A bad day at the office is not the day to give up the job and radically change direction. In good space we can look at recurrent issues.

2. When making decisions within the Ignatian context, we have at least two realistic options in front of us which are morally good. The key here is realism. Our inner world and the outer world must converge. There's no point wanting to study physics at college if I haven't previously shown a potential aptitude in this area. There's no point wanting to play rugby for Ireland or Munster if I'm seventy years old! Before weighing up the choices I need to ask myself if I am being realistic. If not, I should start looking at other options.

3. Gathering data is the next step. If I'm applying for a teaching post in a school, have I looked at the website? Have I understood the ethos of the school? Do I know if the job is permanent or temporary? If I'm building a house, I need to get a realistic idea of costs and the time it will take. Gathering all relevant

data and being open to it until the last minute seems obvious, but not everybody does it. It's easy for ego and pride to take over. A person won't consider new data because a decision was already made, and doesn't want to seem weak by going back on a decision already made, even if going ahead is to omit essential new data, and undermine the original project! We can't be too careful when gathering data, especially as we live in such a fast-changing world. Putting our head in the sand will eliminate us early on in the race. Networking and conversing with the stakeholders are an important part of the process. When Mr Bloomberg decided to quit the US presidential race, he remarked in his speech that: 'I'm a believer in using data to inform decisions.'[30] He added, rather jocosely, that while he was Mayor of New York he respected the 'In God we trust' sentiment, but expected City Hall employees to bring data to work. Ignatius would be proud! Data and trust in God!

4. Self-knowledge cannot be underestimated when making decisions. Ignatius learned this from bitter experience. He was aware that we all have negative energies that drive some of our decisions. That's the reason one of the purposes of the Spiritual Exercises is to help us become aware of and eliminate forces that lead us in the wrong direction. Therefore, I have to do some serious questioning of why I am making this particular decision. Is this really the means to the end? Is this decision really the best? Is it my vanity project? Am I being inspired by anger? Is there a blind spot here? Is this decision inspired by generosity and what's really best for all involved? Can I see the bigger picture? A student decided to go to college to begin medical studies. He sensed that the rest of the family thought he was a bit of an academic dud. He'd show them. By the end of second year, he'd had enough. He quit and started landscape

gardening, which really suited him. The original decision was driven by hurt and insecurity. Each of us needs to make our own best reflective judgements while paying attention to complex ambiguities embedded in the decision.

5. A decision-making experience in Ignatian terms is not an exercise in finding reasons to support a decision I've already made anyway. How many times have people made up their minds beforehand? How many conferences have been publicised as 'decision-making', when in reality the decision was already made? Ignatius wants us to be objective and honest. In order to facilitate this goal, he gives us a number of exercises, and one of the conditions of doing them is genuinely to give both options equal airtime. He wants us to wear each of the possible outcomes objectively, like trying on new clothes in a store, feeling how they fit. When we're satisfied, we purchase. The option that doesn't work for us, just like the ill-fitting clothes, can be rejected.

6. Prayer, for Ignatius, is the linchpin of any decision-making. In a fallible world we can never be certain that we're making exactly the right decision. All we can do is our best. Welcoming God into the process is a way of doing that. Asking God if this decision coincides with his dream for us is a way of moving in the right direction. Does this decision express who I am? Does this decision express my core values? Does this decision really honour my gifts of personality? Of the two options, is this the more generous? When we've made the decision, we bring it back to God for confirmation. We wait and listen, as Sylvia Plath waits for inspiration in 'Black Rook in Rainy Weather': 'The wait's begun again, / The long wait for the angel'.[31] In this case the 'angel' is confirmation of the decision.

---

31 Poem 44, *Sylvia Plath: Collected Poems* (ed. Ted Hughes), London: Faber & Faber, 1981.

CHAPTER NINE

PATHWAYS TO A DECISION

For Ignatius there are six ways that can help lead to a decision. Feelings, reason and imagination are part of the decision-making process, with an emphasis on one or another depending on the particular exercise he puts before us. In practice they can all overlap.

1. The first way of arriving at a decision is when we have no doubt whatsoever that we're doing the right thing. Our inner world and the outer world converge. A person might say that they always wanted to be a teacher. They never wanted to be anything else. Anybody looking in from the outside might say that the person was a born teacher with the ideal personality for the job. The person also has the required academic qualifications to enter college. All other things being equal, this is the path for the person to pursue. There is no turning back, and more importantly, there is no doubt. Ignatius gives two scriptural examples. He refers to St Paul's conversion on the road to Damascus where Paul had an epiphany moment that left him in no doubt where his future lay. He was absolutely certain. He had found what he was looking for. Ignatius also recalls St Matthew's response to Jesus' call. That was it, no further discernment was required. While some do have the 'no doubt' experience it is not usually the norm and most people have to

resort to the more common methods of decision making.

2. The second way to a decision involves the discernment of spirits, sifting through feelings, as outlined earlier. In this method we pay attention to our affectivity. How do I feel about option A having spent a few days mulling it over? How do I feel about option B having spent a few days mulling it over? Am I experiencing different feelings? Am I more attracted to one option than the other? Is a pattern emerging where option A seems to be the preferred option? Am I really trying both options on for size?

Ignatius had to make a decision about which rules of poverty he wanted for the Society of Jesus. It was a choice between strict poverty without a fixed income or a more mitigated poverty. The problem arose in the context of managing and maintaining church buildings. At that time, even the Franciscans and other religious orders had made some exceptions to their poverty rules in order to accommodate appropriate financial arrangements for the upkeep of churches. Ignatius traces his decision-making process in his diary. He writes down the pros and cons. He puts aside forty days to discern prayerfully about the matter. He records his feelings. For thirty-nine days he was happy with where the decision was going. Strict, unmitigated poverty was his preferred choice. His decision was consistently confirmed by a pattern of consolation.

On the final day disaster struck. He went into a tailspin of the most intense desolation. He was making the wrong decision. Was he to start the process all over again? He refused to begin again. He was experienced enough to recognise that when he was in consolation during the previous thirty-nine days, he was happy with his decision of strict poverty. He used his own principles to discern spirits. When in consolation it is the good spirit who's in the driving seat, giving the counselling.

In desolation it is the bad spirit, who can't be trusted, who's in the driving seat, giving the counselling. Therefore, adhering to his own guidelines for the discernment of spirits, Ignatius concluded that the decision made in good space was the way to go. This also illustrates that when a decision is made in good space, it is not to be reversed in a time of desolation, bad space. Stick with the resolution made under the guidance of the good spirit.

Another example may help to highlight other aspects of discernment in this context. Patricia is a popular music teacher in a secondary school. She is married with four children. She and her husband have a property by the sea. A family custom has evolved whereby they always spend the Easter weekend at their seaside property. Such is Patricia's popularity as a talented musician, the parish priest asks her if she would consider taking charge of the music for the Easter liturgy in her home parish. Patricia is chuffed to be asked and she imagines the kudos and adulation that will result if she does a good job which she is confident of doing. She sees lots of advantages.

However, following Ignatius's advice about being objective and in a space of equilibrium she decides that she won't accept the offer immediately. She will think it through. A choice between two options is facing her – Easter liturgy or seaside holiday. She will pray and think about it and reflect on the different feelings that come to the surface. She has enough self-knowledge to realise that she enjoys the spotlight. She remembers how, when she was at college, she would volunteer for anything going. She remembers how her volunteering at different times took its toll and she had to withdraw from what she was doing. At times she asked herself why she was so driven. She concluded that she needed the applause and approval of others to make up for her lack of self-confidence.

Like a lot of people she knew, she also found it difficult to say 'no' as she felt she was letting people down and others might think she was just being selfish. It was easier to say 'yes' than to say 'no'. She could say 'no' to the parish priest, but could she live with the guilty feelings that would follow? After all, wouldn't the more generous thing be to help out the parish? What would her peers at school think if they found out she refused the parish priest? She'd be the talk of the town! As Patricia is able to identify her feelings, she's coming to realise that she would like to do the decent thing by helping out the parish priest, but she's also realising that her decision is being inspired by self-centred concerns. Her inclination is to do the good thing for the reasons that would feed her ego. The bad wolf is lurking. At least a pattern is emerging where saying 'yes' to the Easter liturgy is concerned. For Ignatius decisions are to be inspired by generosity, they're not meant to serve our ego and pride. In this situation the bad spirit is also exploiting Patricia's vulnerabilities.

What happens next? As suggested by Ignatius Patricia sets about gathering more data while listening to her conflicting feelings. She follows Ignatius's advice and shares what's on her mind with her husband rather than keeping it a secret like the enemy of our human nature suggests. This is also a good way to widen the data pool as Ignatius would wish. Her husband knows well how his wife operates. He points out that given how hard she works she'll be exhausted by Easter anyway. Experience has consistently demonstrated that she's frayed at the edges by the time Easter comes around. She doesn't need a major undertaking during Easter, especially in light of the fact that the final term is going to be longer than usual. He points out how important the seaside holiday is for nurturing family life; as a family they prioritise family activities. As a mother and a wife she is already committed to family responsibilities. She doesn't have a responsibility to the parish to provide liturgical music.

Patricia brings all of her feelings and what she's learned from her husband's feedback to prayerful reflection. She's still feeling conflicted. She lives with her conflicting feelings for a few days and then begins to notice that going on the family weekend seems to fit better than the other option. The more her feelings surface, the more she's finding peace in honouring her responsibilities to her family, even if she's dreading saying 'no' to the parish priest. The penny drops that wanting to do the liturgy is the enemy of her human nature disguised as an angel of light. The bad wolf is good at the disguise business. Wanting to do the liturgy is driven more by pride, whereas wanting to holiday with the family is driven by love. She asks God to confirm her decision as Ignatius would have wished. She gets back to the parish priest, thanking him for the opportunity; at least for this year she knows that it would be more generous to honour her family commitments. It's a generous decision even if it is difficult. Patricia has confronted the enemy and robustly decided to do the opposite of what he suggested. Ignatius would be pleased!

If we return to the earlier account of how Richard Malloy discovered his Jesuit vocation, we see this second route to a decision at work. It dawned on him that he was getting more peace and satisfaction from serving in a care facility than from nights out partying with his fellow students. Ignatius, therefore, is asking us to pay attention to our feelings, thoughts and desires, because that's where we will potentially find the place where our desires and God's desires for us will coincide.

3. If a decision has still not been arrived at, Ignatius suggests a very practical exercise involving pen and paper (or, these days,

laptop). In this exercise reason rather than emotion is the guiding force. There are two options, A and B. Ignatius suggests taking each of the two options separately. Take out a sheet of paper. Draw a line down the middle. At the top of the left-hand column, write down Advantages (Pros), and in the right-hand column Disadvantages (Cons). Do the same for option B. We do this, of course, making sure that we are in good space, are impartial, really want to make the best decision which we will bring back to God in prayer for confirmation. When we have written down the pros and cons we analyse them, weighing up the different reasons. It's not numbers we're interested in but quality. I may have five advantages and one disadvantage, but the one disadvantage may carry the most weight. We carefully scrutinise everything making sure we have left nothing out.

Ignatius includes a caveat. Suppose I have an offer of a job in an inner-city school or in a prestigious boarding school. On my Pros list for the boarding school, I include the swimming pool and the excellent haute cuisine. Both of these items are attractive in any working environment and good in themselves. Who wouldn't want to have them? Ignatius, however, would not regard them as compelling reasons for making a choice: 'I must come to a decision because of weightier motives and not because of any sensual inclination' (SE, 182). This is a practical illustration of Ignatius's desire that decisions are motivated by the wish to reach out to others as generously as possible rather than self-gratification. All other things being equal, Ignatius would be disappointed if the only two reasons for my rejection of the inner-city job were the two perks in the boarding school! If my special talent is my ability to teach educationally disadvantaged young people, Ignatius would protest if I let food and swimming get in the way. This is the 'Principle and Foundation' in action.

In a similar way I may have a pet project that's good in itself and a service to the community. I may need to clarify in my own mind whether I'm doing it as a vanity project or because the project is an expression of my generosity. If not, I could work on my motivation. For Ignatius the quality and motivation for any decision are significant. However, we don't live in a perfect world, so we do the best we can within our limitations as we move gradually towards fuller personal integration. French writer André Gide said that the stars, like ideals, are unreachable, but they guide us on our way. Ideals challenge us to grow into who we are.

4. If a decision has not been made using these three methods, Ignatius has three more tricks up his sleeve where we use our imaginative powers. Having had some limited military experience, his attention to detail and thoroughness knew no bounds. So, the next way to a decision is to imagine someone I don't know struggling with the same decision. Ignatius deliberately stresses that I don't know the person because he's trying to protect the value of impartiality. If the person I'm imagining is my partner, my mother or someone else known to me, my partiality might be compromised.

I sit down with this person, who tells me their story and opens their heart to me. I listen carefully to the words and the body language. I may ask questions for clarification. 'Have you ever considered this aspect of what you're trying to decide?' I make other discreet enquiries to build the complete picture. I put the person's impartiality to the test. Then I imagine the conclusion of the conversation and what I would say to that person by way of advice. One of the purposes of this imaginary conversation is to help highlight my own conscious or unconscious biases. Having communicated to the person what I would recommend, Ignatius tells us go and do the same ourselves.

5. If by this time a decision has still not been made Ignatius has two more imaginative exercises up his sleeve, which have a common theme: 'If you had your life to live over again, what would you do differently?' The first of the two final scenarios is my deathbed. If I were on my deathbed, what decision would I make? People close to death have a different take on what really matters and what is trivial. This exercise has the potential to flush out our motivation, clarify values and get rid of what Ignatius calls 'disordered affections' – inclinations towards what's not good for us – so that I make a decision guided by the good spirit, a concept which is the very core of Ignatian spirituality.

6. The final way to a decision, if we're not completely worn out at this stage, is to engage with the imagery of Ignatius's dramatic grandeur. We are before the Judgment seat of God on the Last Day. We're summoned to give an account of our life. The central question is: 'What would I have wanted to have decided while I had the opportunity?' This is really putting it up to us and broadening the horizons of our decisions.

Finally, the decision has been made! There is one final step left before translating the decision to action. Ideally, we return to God in prayer and ask for his confirmation if we still have time. You'd think we'd have done enough at this stage! If time doesn't permit, it may be best to carry on anyway, as long as there is no overwhelming sense of unease or any other factors preventing the implementation of the decision.

In order to assess if confirmation of our decision is forthcoming, once again we pay attention to our feelings. Am I in consolation? I can judge that by where I am being drawn. I could be at peace and feeling confident. That's a good sign. I could be feeling anxious and uneasy at the prospect of change but at the core of my being I'm feeling confident. I'm happy that I can manage the challenges. Past experience has confirmed that. I'm peacefully drawn to the new project. That sounds like consolation and confirmation.

Consolation doesn't always mean 'nice feelings'. The real way of judging is where I am being drawn, despite uncomfortable feelings on the surface, like the wife of the stroke patient, referred to in Chapter 6 on the Examen of consciousness. In spite of her obvious discomfort she kept faith with her husband because of her deep-down conviction that that was the right thing to do. Many of us can identify moments in life where we travelled into the unknown because in our heart of hearts we thought it was for the best and we had the courage not to let fear, uncertainty, doubt, discouragement or anything else overwhelm us.

However, how are we to assess if our decision has not been confirmed? Again, we pay attention to our feelings. It may be the case that I don't do change well, for example. The decision just doesn't fit, at least for now. Perhaps I'm overwhelmed by paralysing fear. Perhaps previous experiences have confirmed that the decision I've made simply won't work for me because it will be too difficult and more than my physical and mental faculties can tolerate. I'm also aware that straining beyond my capacities is too risky, and that it's more prudent to remain where I can manage, even though I may be under-achieving. As we saw earlier, Fr Gerald O'Mahony SJ reminds us that it's easier to recover from under-achieving than it is if the branch snaps. It's not worth taking the risk to find out. I may be missing out but there's too much else at stake, especially my mental health. Perhaps at a future time this decision may be the right one. This sounds like the decision has not been confirmed. There are anxieties and personality factors that need to be respected. In this context it seems best to accept peacefully that this is not the right decision at this time. Perhaps somewhere down the line, some professional support could help with some of the underlying emotional and other issues. As the underlying peace, expected as a sign of confirmation, is clearly absent, it seems best to stay put.

Ignatian decision-making can easily be remembered by recalling the four Ds.

DESIST	Stop what you're doing. Find good space. Equilibrium like weighing scales.
DELIBERATE	Reflect on feelings. Think about reasons. Gather data.
DECIDE	How am I feeling? What am I thinking? Choose. Bring choice to God.
DO	Time to act.

OASIS MOMENTS
– SLAKING THE THIRST

Anybody who has walked through barren, arid terrain in the heat of the day will appreciate how essential it is to find wells along the way in order to slake their thirst. A combination of exercise and intense heat soon leads to dehydration. Many pilgrims on their way to Santiago de Compostela in Spain understand these challenges, especially as they walk through the arid landscape between Burgos and León. In a similar way, as we make our way through life, there are moments when our life is like a desert and we need to stop at the first oasis to fill up with water.

Many of us are concerned about work-life balance in a socio-economic environment where we are run off our feet, working every hour that God sends, and at the end of it all still find it challenging to put a roof over our heads. It often feels overwhelming. Relationships can be put under strain. The quality of family life can suffer. It can be more attractive to engage with virtual acquaintances than the people around us, especially in a culture where instant and frequent affirmation is the norm and where we don't want to miss out. We experience the pressure but are often not sure what to do. Within a family there may be a variety of schedules; children at school, study, choir and games, while parents may work irregular hours, have a long and tiring commute or work night shifts. The idea of a common meal such as dinner may be unsustainable, even though it may be the most important event of the day for facilitating quality family life. Constant exposure to a variety of stimuli is simply not good for us. Social media boundaries are important. Slowing-down time is essential for destressing and recovering our mental equilibrium.

Balancing commitments and priorities is never going to be easy. We're always going to play catch-up. But for our own sanity and peace, some intentional practices are necessary to support our priorities. Finding a balance means making compromises with ourselves. Perhaps we don't need to dust under the bed every day, unless of, course, we're allergic to dust mites or other such nuisances! Not everything needs to look spick and span every second of the day. There are those of us who can easily forget that a home is for living in, not a museum for the living. We need to forget about keeping up with others! There are more important areas in life in which to invest our energies. Returning to Ignatius's 'Principle and Foundation', it can be helpful to ask ourselves what exactly it looks like in our own particular lives. Within my unique context, what are my priorities? What means am I using? Ignatius's wisdom is quite simple. If we don't know what our priorities are, our energies will be unfocused and we'll become tired. We'll be working out of a vague plan where we're not realising what we really hope for and using up precious psychic energy in the process. This in turn will generate anxiety which will further drain our energies. This is one of the areas where Ignatian guidelines can really come into their own.

Taking stock of our lives is sometimes referred to as a 'retreat', which is an oasis time on the path of life. Retreats of one kind or another are an intrinsic part of student life in many secondary schools. They are an opportunity for young people, under the guidance of experienced leaders, to reflect on their lives, learn from them, and progress to the next stage. They involve meditation, interpersonal exercises and other practices to support their relationships and to get a sense of what God is like. Taking this kind of time out can give students life skills to help them cope. Retreats can give focus and direction to life, as we saw in Chapter 2 with the student who had just completed the Quo Vadis Pilgrimage Retreat.

Many, for obvious reasons, feel they don't have the time or opportunity for the oasis moment. However, the oasis moment can come in various guises. It may include a regular walk around the block, the object of which is to debrief after a few stressful days. It could be a more formal event, such as an hour in the evening with others on one day of the week, over a short period of time, nourishing our spirituality. It could be yoga or mindfulness to slow us down and regain perspective. It could include learning more about the practices of other traditions that could enhance our own spirituality.

As was mentioned in connection with the Examen of Consciousness, one of the purposes of prayer is to allow God a window of opportunity to comfort us. The oasis moments are the means by which we open the window. God enjoys our company. We see that in the Adam and Eve story. In the cool of the evening God would meet Adam and Eve on his stroll until the day came when they went into hiding. How disappointed God was that their evening chats had come to an end and that his two favourite people in the whole world had decided to reject the offer of friendship. How gutted God must have felt, having taken the risk of giving himself only to have his offer of friendship rejected.

An oasis moment may be as simple as a short visit to a monastery to spend time in the church, join in the prayers of the monks and nuns, have a cup of coffee in the café, all the while taking in the prayerful peace of the location. Sometimes it helps to buy a small memento as a reminder and as a trigger to sustain what was felt during the visit. An oasis moment could be as simple as a stroll on the beach or in the woods. Natural locations have a way of lifting the spirits. Ignatius reminds us to have a bag of tricks up our sleeve to deal with desolation, times of bad mood. Such oasis moments are invaluable.

Oasis moments can include other activities and places: pattern days, holy wells, mass rocks, local pilgrimages or further afield. Many people take time out, if they're fortunate enough, to spend some time walking to Santiago de Compostela. The structure of the experience allows time to focus on personal and other issues. For some it can be a time for making a life-changing decision. There was one person whose job was to down-size companies. He recounted how despondent his job made him feel, because he was conscious that each downsizing meant devastation for a family. A breadwinner was left unemployed with all the painful disruption that that caused for the whole family. His job stressed him out to the point where he resigned. He decided to do something about his desolation. He took to the road, saying goodbye to his family, to make the pilgrimage to Santiago. During the pilgrimage he was inspired by the good spirit to turn his life around. His new-found consolation led him to set up a company that creates jobs. An unusual example of Ignatian *agere contra*, an about turn. It was the oasis moment that helped him focus on his real priorities and his true self. He had found peace in achieving his heart's desire. He found out how to concretise Ignatian goals in his life. He made a courageous decision that turned out to be a blessing!

Another type of 'retreat' is welcoming the opportunity to spend time in the service of people whose life experience is different from your own. To prepare for this kind of experience it's important to prepare beforehand under the guidance of competent leaders. After the experience, following the Ignatian model, it's essential to reflect. It's helpful to share the experience with others as a pathway to further action. Reflective questions provoke further thought and action: 'How will these few days change my attitude to life?' 'What will I do as a consequence?' There's nothing like listening to the story of a homeless person at first hand to allow us to recognise a wounded person and not a statistic. Such epiphany moments have the potential to change the trajectory of a person's life. They begin to see that an occupation is more about job satisfaction than anything else, and that 'selving' is what life is about – identifying and putting our gifts at the service of others as an expression of our gratitude and praise to God.

If time and finances allow, other pilgrimages such as going to Lourdes can strengthen the spirit. Lourdes gives a special welcome to those who are unwell in body or mind. Many give up their holiday time to volunteer as helpers serving those who require a lot of support. You'll often find them at the end of a long hard day, sitting in the dark near the grotto, with no other sound but the rushing waters of the River Gave and no other smell but the burning of candles. Ignatius's guidelines remind us that God's humble and gentle presence is there, comforting and strengthening all those who have come to the waters seeking to slake their thirst.

Bathing in the waters at Lourdes is particularly faith-filled as long as we are willing to put our preconceptions, prejudices and squeamishness aside. It's an experience that requires courage and humility. It can be a long wait in the queue, providing plenty of opportunities to back out. But waiting in the queue is an oasis moment in itself. We're in solidarity with people from all walks of life, the strong and the weak, the healthy and the unwell, young and old, rich and poor, those broken by life and those for whom it's a constant battle. This is life's field hospital. What holds this chain of frail humanity together is faith and hope, either strong or weak, doubtful or searching. All human life is there, evoking Isaiah's encouraging invitation: 'Come, all you who are thirsty, come to the waters', and echoing Jesus' words to the Samaritan woman at the well: 'Whoever drinks the water I give them will never thirst.'

As we approach the water, all the roles we play in life, the disguises we wear, the posturing we adopt, the layers that protect us from the world are stripped from us. The damp loincloth preserves a modicum of modesty while giving a whole new meaning to Job's 'Naked I came from my mother's womb, and naked I will depart. The Lord gave and the Lord has taken away; may the name of the Lord be praised' (Job 1:21). The sense of solidarity with the human community is reinforced by the quasi-nakedness. All pretence has now been stripped away. This is human life at its most basic, without the props to bolster ourselves up. The privileged location and the faith context make this a very different experience from preparing to dip in the Blue Lagoon or the local swimming pool. The Lourdes Bath is prayer in motion. It's acknowledging our existential poverty and the gratuity of God, and highlighting our identity as a 'person-in-relationship'. It's a moving and challenging prayer. It's a real reinforcement of Ignatius's 'Principle and Foundation', where he emphasises that we are from God and that our mission in life is to walk with and serve God's friends, especially those who can't fend for themselves.

Then the moment we've been waiting for arrives. We walk down the steps into the mysterious waters of the ice-cold spring water bubbling up from the depths of the earth. Adult volunteers are there to make sure we don't slip or fall. As at Baptism we're plunged into the water while reciting the prescribed prayers. It's all over in a matter of seconds. We emerge. We're not allowed to use a towel as we dress ourselves and return from this unusual oasis with a spring in our step to take up where we left off, nourished by the witness and support of others.

It is sometimes the case that people have been cured in Lourdes for reasons that are not understood. These events are called miracles – like sacraments, a privileged meeting place with the healing God. But other miracles occur, the deepening sense of solidarity with the rest of the human family, especially those who are ill and for whom life is a tough struggle where multiple painful challenges are the daily lot. There's a sense of: 'We're all in this together', and there's no point in pretending otherwise by denying the very core of our identity – a person-in-relationship.

Another person had to deal with a deeply traumatising family tragedy. The rhythm of a Lourdes pilgrimage was their saviour. They could empathise in particular with the poverty and struggles of Bernadette Soubirous on the pilgrim visits to the places associated with the visionary when she was a young girl. The person was encouraged at the thought of the Mother of Jesus at the grotto. The regular rhythm of the Rosary was the background music of the pilgrim day. But the 'spiritual' was balanced by the 'craic' at the hotel in the evenings. For those troubled by life, Lourdes can be a real oasis, strengthening a person for the return home, where, as Ignatius reminds us, there will be other days of desolation, bad space. The memories of the oasis moment can strengthen us. The oasis moments can be 'The waters of hope / in the expectation / Of Transfiguration'.[32] The transfiguration arising from that oasis moment is when all those disjointed and subconscious fragments of our lives suddenly take on a pattern that gives us hope and faith, which can lead to good space, what Ignatius would call spiritual consolation.

Finding oasis moments is primarily using our creativity to find what fits and what works. Oasis moments – whatever their form – are essential to healthy living and don't need to be dramatic gestures. Think in terms, perhaps, of a prolonged Examen where there may be a little more to be thinking and praying about. A short time reading or listening to nourishing podcasts may also give us the encouragement we need. An oasis moment might be listening to inspiring music driving to work, or simply quiet time in a local church admiring the stained-glass windows, the icons or other images. It may be the parish novena. There are many possibilities. It's a question of finding what fits, because a taste for 'holy' practices is very much a personal matter. We need to find something that resonates with us, so it may be a case of trial and error until we find what we're looking for. It may also be a case of *agere contra*, where we have to make a choice between settling down to watch TV ten minutes later so that we can give priority to an oasis experience to clear the clutter of head and heart. It can be more attractive to lounge on the sofa as a couch potato, but the oasis moment will serve our True Self.

We don't always need to take the lead where oasis moments are

32 Jim Maher, 'Lourdes Bath'.

concerned because God sometimes literally comes to our rescue, but oasis moments facilitate his arrival, so it's best not to abandon them. It can happen that we're in bad space, in Ignatian desolation, going around in circles, and then, for no logical reason, we start reading something that coincidentally hits the spot, or we meet somebody who says exactly the right thing, and our desolation begins to lift. Encouragement is restored. How did God know that that's exactly what I needed to hear?

Other experiences may have the same result. Such experiences are not infrequent and a regular Examen will bring them to light. Albert Einstein used to remark that coincidences are moments when God chooses to communicate with us anonymously. Some apparently coincidence moments are like finding the oasis in the desert. Coincidences are not to be dismissed lightly. They may well be God's direct intervention for the better in our lives. We need to discern by asking: 'Where is this experience leading me?' Coincidences are similar to minor miracles where God's presence is evident. Tread lightly because God is here. Such experiences confirm God's friendship. God does give signs to those who have eyes to see. Our planet is holy ground where we cooperate with God in realising its transfiguration. We are part of Someone bigger than ourselves, who loves us in a way that's beyond our comprehension. Even though we have come a long away from our original evolution the story is not over yet, as we move towards our fulfilment as God intended.

CONCLUSION

The 2003 film *Cowboys and Angels*, a particular favourite among young people, was filmed on location in Limerick. It's a coming-of-age story about two young men, Shane and Vincent. During the voice-over at the beginning, Shane is heard asking a number of questions: 'Have you ever felt that life was passing you by? Did you ever feel like there was something missing? If you knew what that something was, would you know where to look for it?' These questions in particular echo Ignatius's 'Principle and Foundation' about identity and much of the content of this book.

Coincidentally, the opening sequence of the film, after the credits, was shot outside the former Jesuit church and school in Limerick after the transfer to the Dooradoyle campus. If you take a close look you will see a former member of the Jesuit community walking past the church, unaware that he was being filmed.

Shane is a naive country lad from Doon. His dream of going to college comes to an end with the sudden death of his father in a road traffic accident. To support his family financially he becomes a clerk at the Department of Agriculture in Limerick city. It's clear his heart isn't in the job. Jerry, a bachelor, who had worked at the same office for forty-seven years, since he was a teenager, dropped dead during his retirement party in a local pub. Earlier in the film during a conversation with Jerry, Shane asks why he stayed in a job he hated for so long. Jerry replies: 'I was afraid, son. It's as simple as that. I hadn't the balls to do anything different.' Sadly, Jerry (played by Frank Kelly, who also played the infamous 'Fr Jack' in *Father Ted*) spent his life locked in a self-imposed prison of fear and cowardice.

Shane finds accommodation in a city-centre flat with Vincent, a flamboyant and outgoing gay student at the Limerick College of Art and Design. As events unfold in a comic and unexpected way, they form a warm friendship and Vincent brings Shane out of his introversion. As the opening voice-over confirms, there is something missing at the core of Shane's life. His talent for art is gradually revealed. His job becomes increasingly at odds with his heart's desire to become an artist like Vincent. Eventually he works up the courage to quit his day job and sends an application to the College of Art. He's going to realise his dream of creating beauty for beauty's sake. During the voice-over at the end, Shane triumphantly asserts his new-found freedom when he confidently affirms: 'I've found my voice. Show me how to use it.' Shane had embraced his identity. He had come home to himself. He had met the longing of his heart. Our mentor in this book, Ignatius of Loyola, would have applauded his decision.

Like Ignatius and Richard Malloy, whose vocation stories were recounted, it took a circuitous route for Shane to discover what the real desire of his heart was. For Richard Malloy, the cannon-ball experience was a fall that left him in hospital, and for Shane it was Jerry's fear-filled life, among other things.

Ignatius wants us to pay attention to our inner self so that we speak with our own voice. Many other voices, which do not have our interests at heart, compete for our attention. It takes courage to speak with our own voice – there will be many who won't approve of what we say because it doesn't conform to the unexamined assumptions of the conventional wisdom that influences our culture. We live against the background of cacophonous voices telling us to do this, that or the other in order to be a somebody. How often do we buy in to the lie? The poet Emily Dickinson humorously puts somebodies in their place when she says: 'How dreary – to be – Somebody! / How Public – like a Frog / To tell one's name – the livelong June – / To an admiring Bog!'[33]

Consider the pressure it puts on young people, in particular, who feel that if they don't conform to stereotypical images of how to be a man or a woman, they are failures. Ignatius himself was aware of this from his own first-hand experience. His idea of happiness and success was to carve out a niche for himself among the perceived movers and shakers until his cannon-ball experience opened his eyes to what he would have been missing out on by being someone other than he really was. The cannon ball shattered not only his legs but his illusions as well. To express ourselves with our own distinctive voice usually doesn't happen in a dramatic way as it did for Ignatius. It can be a slow, arduous process, requiring patience, courage, self-acceptance, the capacity to forgive ourselves and others and to move beyond unhealthy guilt and shame that can weigh heavily on our shoulders and prevent us living gracefully in the present. Ignatian wisdom can facilitate the process, especially his guidelines for mood interpretation and his Examen of Consciousness prayer, so that we can sift out the voices that bring us down and lie to us, making us feel as if we were of little value.

Ironically, the Covid-19 pandemic challenged some of our assumptions about the way we normally live our lives and the things we take for granted. In a similar way, the Camino to Santiago de Compostela challenges the unnecessary baggage we carry round. Life is often simpler and more joyful when pared back to the basics in the company of others. Many return from their Camino with good intentions about living a simpler and more wholesome life. Sadly, their dreams often perish due to the pressures of daily life or because they planned to bite off more than they could chew. Sometimes small really is beautiful, and simple

---

33 Poem 260, *The Poems of Emily Dickinson*, R.W. Franklin (ed.), Cambridge, MA: Belknap Press, 1999.

steps can go a long way in life transformation. Sitting on the banks of restful waters during oasis moments is helpful, because it provides the opportunity to take stock and satisfy the thirst of the spirit.

A small group of students was walking to Santiago de Compostela, having set off from St-Jean-Pied-de-Port, the French town at the foot of the Pyrenees. On the eighth day the students arrived discouraged at one of the hostels. It was time to give up and go home. They were in a bad mood, experiencing what Ignatius calls desolation. During the course of a good pick-me-up meal it became apparent that they were carrying too much in their backpacks. They were well-intentioned setting out but didn't quite grasp that this was a challenging physical pilgrimage with no opportunity for excess baggage. Their mums had packed tubes of sunblock Factor 50 for the first few days, then sunblock Factor 30 for the days after that, and other lotions and potions to deal with the effects of sun and other dermatological issues. The students had packed their party jeans, shirts and shoes for what they thought would be wild parties at night! Various cosmetics and toiletries were included. Gadgets of one kind or another were taking up precious space and adding to the weight. It was no wonder they were fed up. On the following morning there was a merciless trawl of the backpacks to remove and send home all unnecessary items. Three weeks later they arrived in Santiago safe, sound, ebullient and wiser. Blistered feet and weighty backpacks were the cannon balls that got the students to re-examine their priorities.

As we've seen, Vincent asks a profound question: 'Did you ever feel like there was something missing? If you knew what that something was, would you know where to look for it?' Perhaps at different stages of life we can relate to this question. Ignatius of Loyola helped many people to deal with this question in an imaginative and creative way. His strategies, outlined in this book, are a helpful way of engaging with the most important questions of all so that, like Vincent, we can say: 'I've found my voice', or, with Gerard Manley Hopkins, cry out: '*What I do is me: for that I came.*'

In summary, Ignatian spirituality wholeheartedly embraces life in all its fullness. It's extraordinarily optimistic and life-affirming. It invites us to open our hearts to God's friendship in the variety of ways it's presented to us in the ordinary circumstances of life in the spirit of Patrick Kavanagh's poem 'The Great Hunger', when he writes, 'God is in the bits and pieces of Everyday – / A kiss here and a laugh again'. It challenges us to discover the dreams that God has planted in our hearts, which are expressed through our own distinctive and unique voices. Ignatius teaches us how to become our 'self'. He reminds us that when we 'selve' we give praise and gratitude to God. He emphasises that true happiness comes from openness to God and others while expressing the deepest desires of the heart. He leaves us a legacy of waymarks to make the most of our human experience in all its many dimensions. Echoing Frost's poem about making a choice on a woodland path, the Ignatian pathway is the one that 'has made all the difference' for so many.

BIBLIOGRAPHY

Aschenbrenner, George. *Stretched for Greater Glory*. Chicago, IL: Loyola Press. 2004.

Boulvin, Yves. *100 chemins pour découvrir Dieu dans la vie de tous les jours*. France: Éditions des Béatitudes. 2013.

Byron, William, SJ. *Answers from Within: Spiritual Guidelines for Managing Setbacks in Work*. Dublin: Veritas Publications. 2010.

Corbishley, Thomas, SJ. *The Spiritual Exercises of St Ignatius of Loyola*. London: Burns & Oates Limited. 1963.

Dreamer, Oriah Mountain. *The Call: Discovering Why You are Here*. London: HarperCollins. 2003.

Fleming, David L. *Contemporary Reading of the Spiritual Exercises*. St Louis, MO: The Institute of Jesuit Sources. 1980.

Gallagher, Timothy. *Handbook for Spiritual Directors*. Kindle Edition, 24 April 2017.

Loyola, Ignatius, Trans. Joseph Munitz. *Personal Writings*. London: Penguin, 1996.

Malloy, Richard G., SJ. *Spiritual Direction: A Beginner's Guide*. Maryknoll, NY: Orbis Books. 2017.

Manney, Jim. *What Do You Really Want?* Huntington, IN: Our Sunday Visitor. 2015.

Martini, Carlo-Maria Cardinal. *Letting God free us*. Slough and New York, NY: St Pauls and New City Press. 1993.

Meissner, W.W. *Ignatius of Loyola, The Psychology of a Saint*. New Haven, CT, and London: Yale University. 1992.

Nault, Jean-Charles, OSB. *The Noonday Devil*. San Francisco, CA: Ignatius Press. 2015.

Phillips, Catherine. *Gerard Manley Hopkins*. Oxford and New York, NY: Oxford University Press. 1986.

Puhl, Louis J. *The Spiritual Exercises of St. Ignatius*. Chicago, IL: Loyola University Press. 1951.

Stack, Tom. *No Earthly Estate*. Dublin: Columba Press. 2004.

Tellechea Idigoras, José Ignacio, Trans. Cornelius Michael Buckley SJ. *Ignatius of Loyola – The Pilgrim Saint*. Chicago, IL: Loyola Press. 1994.

Thibodeaux, Mark. *God's Voice Within*. Kindle Edition, 1 November 2010.

Young, William J. *Letters of St Ignatius of Loyola – Selected and Translated*. Chicago, IL: Loyola University Press. 1959.